Fool's
Paradise

Fool's Paradise
It's Teenage!

Arunmozhi Nambi

PARTRIDGE
A Penguin Random House Company

To order additional copies of this book, contact
Partridge India
000 800 10062 62
orders.india@partridgepublishing.com

www.partridgepublishing.com/india

About the Author

*A*runmozhi Nambi, who is also a teenager, student in VIT, talks about the fun and emotional journey of an Indian teenage boy.

The plot travels with all the different life events encountered by Surya, which showed him the taste of friendship, love and lessons of life.

Hello…!

We all have lived teenage! A man or a woman is said to be adorable and fresh as babies, cute and active as kids, strong and built as young adults, ripe and fighting through the middle ages, wise and childish in the end. Every human's life rises and falls from the beginning to the end. The graph of happiness for a human might look as the outline of a downhill. Ask anybody about their old days, they'll always start with a sigh. That's because their old days were much more magical than their present. Ask them again after a few more months, and they'll refer to the present being the fun one. Day by day, pressure holds on to the life; Day by day everything is put to test; Day by day a man or a woman gets worn out. But, to almost everyone, sometime or the other, magic would've happened. Sometime or the other, life would've been kind. Sometime or the other, they had lived a dream. Unlike to all nature's mysteries, all these incidents, would take place on everyone's teenage. It's the living heaven for the people and the tastiest moment is when we realize how awesome our teenage was, way away from it. It's something everybody would love to relive. It's fresh and active and adventurous; where we'll have nothing to lose and a lot to win.

This is the life story of Surya. Perhaps he was the luckiest teen to ever live on the face of the earth. Luck followed him wherever he went. He was not only the luckiest, but also the smartest one too. Wherever he *goes he was followed by words "Wow! Surya, how are you man!" "Hey, Surya can you sit next to me today?" "Surya, ma'am called you to give a speech", "Surya, they have chosen you as the most stylish badminton player in the state!" "Surya, Surya, Surya" was the name chanted everywhere in the neighbourhood.*

In his school, he was the best loved child. A child loved by the correspondent, principal, teachers and all the children from the small legged kindergarteners to the senior most twelfth graders. Each and every soul loved him. He was praised, adored and followed wherever he went. On the whole this boy was the star of the century! His parents were more than proud for him. They swam across a river called pride. Surya had countless number of friends who knocked his door, more than his mom or dad. He also had a soft place in all the girls' hearts.

His Facebook profile had crossed numerous friends, texted by a million people, gossiped by many, rumoured countless number of times. On the whole he had life on a gold plate. So as I was saying this is the epic story of "Surya, The Awesome Boy" you've ever heard of!

Chapter 1: Surya

I *think that's a good life a boy can get. It's the life each and every teenage boy wants. Even grown-ups need a life like that. Who would not want a life like that? Most of us want it. Basic human character needs it. The fame and popularity and attention and all those success, each and every person in the world wants it. Well, it is also the life Surya himself wanted.*

Most of us have read and heard a phrase "Dreams come true!" even we might have even experienced it, say we got a dream bike, purchased a new video game or got into a famous worldwide college or got a dream job, saw the love of our life, etcetera. At least once in a while we did get our dreams come true. Well, Surya's life is a little bit complicated.

According to the Hindu mythology, they say Lord Brahma writes the fate of each and every person alive. He is the one who decides what fun and sorrow a person gets. Well in Surya's fate, he wrote one too many sorrows, mixed with fun, maybe he wrote it in a state of a Bi-Polar Disorder. Surya's life episodes start with a very happy beginning and then it takes a twist that suddenly turns into a tragedy. This story is about such episodes in Surya's life. It travels in the years where Surya studies in two schools, from his ninth grade to the twelfth grade, where the glorious teenage flourishes. I humbly request the reader to travel into the mind of a teenager. Well, we can't straight away pass to ninth grade in the curriculum. Let's have a quick travel with Surya till his ninth grade.

First let's go to 21ˢᵗ of May 1996. The day Surya started his life journey. Surya was born cute. He had great big eyes that gleamed. He couldn't compete with his brother's complexion. He was dark when compared to his brother Hari. Fate started for Surya who at that moment didn't know anything. Among the people who were amazed with his cuteness, there came a voice "Oh, mommy this baby is black! He's not fair like Hari." Well, good thing that baby Surya couldn't have understood it.

Years passed, Surya started growing, and he did have quite a good childhood. Those times, his family and relatives really loved him. His first ever friend was Pallavi. Surya and Pallavi exchanged toys, played in the streets of their houses and had a lovely childhood. It was right then... at that moment... Pallavi flew to some other place. Surya did not have complete fun. Friendship with Pallavi was short termed, only for nearly six months or so.

Surya joined in the school near the neighbourhood. That was the most popular school in the district, called C.B.W. Surya studied well initially. His marks till the second grade were higher. Surya had a marvellous time in those classes. By June '03 Surya stepped into his third grade. Maybe God thought it's time to start his play with Surya. In Surya's school, by November or December a publisher who's famous for children's books would put a stall. Surya went to the stall and saw the book "Alice in Wonderland". He was attracted by its cover. He badly wanted it the same day. He was aware that the stall stays for three days in the school, but he didn't want to waste time in waiting for the next day and also young Surya didn't have a huge amount of 130 rupees to buy the book! So, off he went to the school opposite to his. It was there his mom worked. Both of the schools were sharing the same ground and it was under the same management of I.E.C., the Indian Electricals Corporation, where Surya's father worked.

Surya went during the lunch break. To his surprise, he was informed that his mother went to an educational office nearby. But his interest to the book didn't stop him. He asked another teacher of the school to call his dad, asking money. Surya's dad arrived by a delay of thirty minutes after the call. Poor guy didn't understand what book it is and why is it needed for. In his busy schedule thinking that it might be an important one, he hurried to offer the money. But he wasn't so sure to hand such a huge sum of money for a boy of just seven years old. The teacher who called Surya's dad was 'so very kind' to accompany Surya for buying the book and to leave him in his class.

With the money received, Surya happily set off to buy the book and read it. He didn't even walk the length of the ground, he ran through it. Finally, Surya and the lady walked into the stall, bought the book, and Surya was to be left in the class. While walking from the stall to the class, Surya's heart leaped with joy. His struggle has finally paid-off, he's got his book! Surya's happiness made his lips stretch from his left-ear to his right-ear. He wanted to show the book to his mom and dad and wanted to show them that he could read English stories!

With this same happiness, he entered his classroom. His classmates were already seated in their places. The class teacher was there too! The lady who came with Surya asked the class teacher to let him inside. The class teacher spoke things in fast English that the seven year old lad couldn't understand. But he did hear the last phrase. It was an earthquake for him. Why? What could be so shocking for a seven year old lad? That too, the words came from his teacher? What could she possibly say?

Well, the teacher said, "Take him to the principal's room."

It indeed is a thunderclap for a small seven year old boy. The principal was the blood-sucking vampire for every child in the primary school. Surya was scared. He didn't know why the teacher had asked him to see the principal. He also didn't know that, he was late for the class by a solid 40 minutes after the lunch break. Surya left his school bag in the class, worrying the teacher, who set out to search for him. It was only when the principal had scolded him, called his brother from class complained about Surya for his misbehaviour, Surya had understood his fault. The day was a terror memory in his tiny mind.

Well people do mistakes, they get caught sometimes and they're punished for it. It happens for each individual. What's so special to talk about this for so long? You may ask. But God had placed his little twist here. Remember the 'kind' lady who accompanied Surya? She was there with him when Surya's principal had scolded him and his brother. But to her, it was a big fault a child had did. She was really angry. After the principal left, she left Surya in his class, and directly went to his mother, to complain about Surya for what had happened. Told you she's a kind lady. She was so kind in telling everything to Surya's mom. Well she was angry too! While reporting it to his mom, she added a little spice to the story. This is the place where hands of God play its duty, she added a few scripts telling, "Surya told me that this was the last day for the sale of books, and he didn't even say that it was a story book! The principal scolded ME for HIS misbehaviour. I had so much anger that I would've slapped him right there."

Surya's mom became furious. She didn't want to hear those words about her son. She was embarrassed. That evening was a time Surya will never forget. Usually, Surya's father would scold him and his mother would console him. But when he saw his mother scolding him for the first time, he broke into tears. Well, after a very long one-way conversation, the family was off to bed by 10:00 pm. Young Surya slept hours before in sadness, ending the day. Wonder what happened to the book that caused all these events? Surya didn't even touch it again.

The incident above is the trailer for what Surya's going to face in his glorious high school years, for whose fun, fate has skipped the rest of the years till his eighth grade free, giving him some gifts that he loved then and there. Half way through summer of 2009, started the Main picture of Surya's life, Directed by the God himself...

Chapter 2: Boarding School

Surya's now a grown up. Well, at least to him. He has completed his eighth grade. He's a teenager now! 13 years old. People had said him 'Teenage is different. All teens are different.' Well as Surya enters teenage, his brother was leaving off it. Surya was pretty excited with this teenage topic. He was happy for his age. We left young Surya sleep crying at seven years. Now let's see how he's grown up.

Let's first try to imagine how our Surya is. Our boy is obviously not prince charming. He wasn't that bad either. He looked good only up to the face. That too, was favoured only by his eyes and smile. Surya did have a little complex on his colour. Well, he was in every possible looks an average scorer. He actually was also plump to his age. Think that's enough for our boy. Let's call him as "Hefty-handsome" to sum it all up.

It was the summer of 2009. The climate though hot, wasn't even felt by Surya. Surya completed his exams, had new friends across the street. Surya felt happy to get into a whole new gang. The children across the street were mostly the same age as Surya. But age doesn't matter when it comes to fun. The street was filled with laugh and joy. All the morning time went in playing cricket, T.V., street shuttle; hilarious talks etc., by the second week of May '09, Surya's family had made a decision to join him in a better school. They've known that for miles around the district, there's no better school than C.B.W. So they've started searching for schools in Chennai. His brother's college was in Chennai too. But after searching and searching for the perfect school, they found one in the outskirts of Chennai. It is called Anand

Krishna Residential School, to be handy, A.K.R.S. Yes, Surya was going for a boarding school. So, with Surya, his father and brother went to visit the school.

"Dad, are we there yet?" asked Surya.

"Not yet dummy, are you seeing any huge building saying Anand Krishna Residential School here?" replied his brother Hari.

"I know genius, but we are walking for half a kilometre from the bus stand! Auto rickshaw's strike is the perfect event for me right now. The school is giving me physical training lessons already." Said Surya, gasping.

"At least you can reduce your weight! You don't want to be like this in your new school."

"Ugh, Dad, are we there or not?"

"Yes Surya, just a few more steps," replied his father.

After the walk, they reached A.K.R.S. The building was more than satisfactory for Surya's dad and Hari. Surya was convinced, only when he heard that the campus was air-conditioned. Surya loved it and he was very happy. Those days, Surya was fantasized with Harry Potter, and he was excited to live like Harry; to live in Hogwarts, in our case A.K.R.S. Surya even day dreamed with him wearing those robes, with a magic wand and walking around the campus of A.K.R.S. performing magic. That day after buying the application, the trio went home.

"How was the school Surya?" asked his mother.

"Nice mom, I'm going to live like Harry!"

"Is it okay for you to be in hostel Surya?"

"Yes mom, what's there in it?"

"There's nothing for me in it. I'm asking for you Surya. We will miss you. I think you will be happier. You'll have the whole day of fun with your friends. It's what you like isn't it?"

"Yes mom, it would be really cool! I know, even I'll miss you. I will miss you all. But it'll be for just few days. Then I'll be okay. It's time to move on mom. I'm a teen now!"

"If you say so, Surya"

There ended the conversation. Surya was happy. He saw the list of things the school had given him. He planned on buying all of them the next day. He couldn't even sleep that night. Days passed and all the things were bought. New uniforms were stitched; but the school stated that there will be an excuse for the first fifteen days. So Surya was happy to wear his casuals. All were packed and Surya started the journey with his mom, dad and Hari.

The car travelled for the seventy two kilometres with different thoughts. The Maruti 800 they were in was filled with all these different emotions. Surya didn't know anything but was excited. Hari was happy that Surya had got into a good school. Surya's father was a bit worried, for he invested an amount of one and a half lakhs of Rupees, thinking whether Surya would come up or not and was praying for him to study well. Surya's mom was a lot worried. She couldn't tolerate leaving both of her sons away from her. She was controlling her tears to make Surya feel good and not to worry.

They reached A.K.R.S. All the formalities were done for leaving Surya in the hostel. Parents were not allowed beyond the doors of the rooms. Surya took both of the big luggage that he bought, the one with dresses and the other with the books. He struggled to take them and keep them in his bed. After keeping the bags Surya sat with his family in the reception. All of them saw a small boy crying desperately, hugging his mom, begging, to take him with her. Surya sighed on seeing the pain of the boy and turned on to look at his dad. To his surprise, he saw his dad crying too.

"What happened dad?" Asked Surya

"Nothing, Surya"

"Say!"

"No… that boy, crying… is too sad." Surya's dad's voice choked.

"Oh don't worry dad, He'll be okay!" Said Surya, not knowing that his father was crying for leaving him in the hostel.

"Parents must leave now. Students are requested to leave to their rooms" Said the warden.

"Bye Dad, you guys can leave now."

"Let's wait Surya. For another five minutes." Surya's father said.

"Okay dad."

"Mom, don't worry, I'll come once in a month. Hari, don't be so happy. I didn't go that far. We'll meet often. I'll visit you in the outing if I get the pass. Dad, they say you can come every weekend and take me out, just come for the first few weeks can you?"

"If they give a chance like that, I'll come for the whole year Surya. You don't worry." His father replied, trembling. Tears rolled from his eyes after he said this. Surya only then realized that his father was crying for leaving him. Only then he felt the sorrow of the Family.

"Okay, Surya, I think we might leave" Said his father, wiping out the tears from his chin.

"Can you wait for five more minutes, dad?" Surya slowly asked. His father could not hold his feelings anymore. He started crying more. He held Surya tightly in his arms. Surya though felt sad, tried to console him.

"It will all be fine dad. Don't worry."

Then after a few minutes of silence, the warden asked Surya's parents to leave the hostel immediately. When Surya's father asked for another five minutes, he said, "I know the feeling sir, don't worry there's phone in the Hostel. The number's been given in the booklet given to you. You can call to him tonight." This encouraged Surya's dad. He felt relieved. Then even with heavy heart, he smiled and bid Surya 'bye'.

Hari and Surya's mom did the same. Surya bid 'bye' and watched the Maruti 800 disappear through the gates of A.K.R.S.

As his family went by, Surya turned back, headed to his room. All the thoughts that went in his mind were, "So that's it. I'm on my own now. I should make my parents feel proud. I should make the money worth it." Saying this, he went inside his dormitory. Hostels of A.K.R.S. are of dorm type. 30 students and a warden stayed in it. Surya's bed was the third. They had a window of two beds. Surya's company was with Ashish. He was the one next to Surya. At first, Surya called for Ashish and greeted him with a Hi. Ashish didn't react well. He didn't even Smile at Surya.

"Okay, that's what I'm going to deal with." Surya sighed.

By 2:30 Surya's parents left. It took till 5:00 for Surya to arrange his clothes and books. There had been an announcement that the principal of A.K.R.S. would be checking all the dorm cupboards and would reward the ones that are neat. So Surya took a keen interest in arranging them neatly. By 5:10 Mrs Saraswati, Principal of A.K.R.S. had arrived to Surya's dormitory. She started seeing all the cupboards. She praised a few cupboards for the neatness. But she didn't even look at Surya's. Surya was a bit disappointed, which he later forgot. It was 5:15. The warden had announced that all Students are to go to the canteen and have their snacks and can go play their favourite sports. Surya was accompanied by Ashish's gang. Nikhil- Ashish's best friend, Abharan, Sanjay, Dhanush.

"*In which school did you study before?*" *asked Nikhil.*

"*I'm from C.B.W.*"

"*C.B.W.! why did you leave such a great school and join here?*" *Sanjay exclaimed.*

"*It was my Parents' idea.*"

"*Fees were cheaper there right?*" *Dhanush quizzed.*

"*Yes. A lot*"

Later, all of them introduced themselves to Surya. Surya felt happy. He didn't even feel sadness on leaving the family that time. That night after dinner, it was Party time in the dormitory. The entire thirty students joined together in Surya and Ashish's compartment. They started with their introduction, went on with some music played by few people, and then they were speaking all about movies, from regional, national to international movies. Surya enjoyed all of it. By 1:30, the warden came and shouted at all the boys to head to their beds. Each of them did so. When Surya saw the warden, only then he was reminded of his father, to call Surya.

"*Did my father call Warden?*"

"*No boy. Now are you going to sleep or not?*" *Replied the warden angrily.*

"*Warden please, let me speak to him just this once.*" *Surya begged.*

"Okay. Just this day I'll let you speak." After which the warden handed over the mobile phone to Surya. Surya called his dad and spoke to him for a few minutes. Surya conveyed to his dad that he was enjoying the school. His dad, who was worried before, felt a bit happier now. He was relieved. Both of them went to sleep happily after the conversation.

Chapter 3: A.K.R.S.

*T*he morning bell in the hostel rang. It was 5:00 am. According to the hostel rules, all students have to get ready for yoga classes at 6:00. Surya woke up early. The new surroundings didn't give him a deep sleep. He woke up in the warden's first call. There he went to the common restroom, brushed, bathed and had on his outfits by 5:30. He waited till the six o'clock bell to strike.

The yoga classes were in the first floor, behind the nurses' station. They walked up the stairs, went to the yoga hall and started doing their activities as instructed by the yoga master. Yoga classes went on till 7:30 and the students returned to their dorms after that. Surya went too. He packed all of his books in the bag and went to the canteen. The breakfast was Idly and Dosa. The food they gave was unbearable. Surya didn't like it. He left almost all of them in the dustbins and off he went to attend his first class in A.K.R.S. He was so happy to find the A.C.s put on and the classroom was cool, literally. He sat alone at first. Ashish was on the next class, 9th A. As his second language was Hindi. Surya's second language was Tamil. Therefore he was in 9th B.

The first bell rang at 8:40. Students began to walk in. The class had fourteen girls and twenty eight boys. Surya sat in the first bench. All the students walked in. by the second bell, Surya's class teacher walked in. he introduced himself to the class.

"Hello, My dear students. I'm your class teacher. The name's Johnson. I'll be taking English classes for this year. You will be attending your first assembly now. After the assembly it'll be English session. So let's have our introductions later. Now off you go for your assembly."

All the students marched away. Assembly in A.K.R.S. is longer than C.B.W. in C.B.W. the assembly comprises of a talk by a student, recent news, thought for the day, announcement, pledge and the national anthem. It took only 20 minutes for an assembly in C.B.W. but in A.K.R.S., the assembly starts with the morning prayer, two of the famous 'Thirukural' with their meaning, two English thoughts, talk by two students, talk by teachers, few exercises as instructed by the physical training master, talk by the principal, announcements, the 'Thamizh Thai Vaazhthu' meaning praising the Goddess Tamil language and finally the national anthem. Each and every student gets tired and would be filled with sweat when the assembly gets over. Moreover it was a daily assembly in A.K.R.S. whereas in C.B.W., it was twice in a week. It was indeed a tiresome assembly in A.K.R.S.

The classes went on smoothly. Surya listened well, made friends too. There were also day-scholars in A.K.R.S. they get a bus trip to school. His first ever day-scholar friend was Vinnie. Vinnie Maria. Surya was reminded of his neighbourhood friends on seeing Vinnie. She was a jovial person. She was an old student of A.K.R.S. She instructed the rules and regulations of the school to him. All went well. She never spelled Surya's name correctly. She would place an 'i' and write it as Suriya. So Surya would always instruct her not to put an 'i'

"How would you like it if I called you 'villie'?" He would say whenever she mistakes on writing his name.

Friendship was fun on classes in A.K.R.S. but the real trouble started by the end of the day. For every student, end of a day at school, means running to their homes. That is the reason why they long for the last bell in the last period. Surya did not long, but he waited for the day to end. But in the last period, after the bell, the teacher instructed that,

"All hostellers must stay. The day-scholars may go."

"Why must we stay and you shall go?" Asked Surya

"We must board the buses. You're staying here that's why." replied Vinnie.

"But... why?"

"What if you board a bus and get away?"

"Huh? Did we pay so much hostel fees to run off? What kind of idiotic system is this?"

"Ask the principal then, now I must go. See you tomorrow. Bye Surya!" said Vinnie and rushed to catch the bus.

Surya waited till the teacher instructed to go. While leaving the class, it was then he remembered how he rushed to his home after school in C.B.W. and saw his mom, brother and dad. It was then he started missing his family. Even though school was over, he was still at school. This increased the missing. He wanted to meet his mom, dad, bro and tell them how the day was, how nice his new friends were, how the teachers were. He never said these stuffs to his parents before. When he wanted to say it, his parents were not there. This broke his heart. He started crying. Poor guy, he became so homesick. He went to his dorm and started crying more. A few minutes later, Ashish came by.

"Surya, what happened?" asked Ashish.

"I miss my family so badly. I want to see them right now." Surya replied. His voice was trembling in his cry.

"Don't worry Surya, even I miss my family. But we should tolerate the pain somehow."

"Why are you here Ashish? Why did you join in a boarding school?"

"My parents fight a lot Surya. They didn't want me or my educations spoil with their fight. So they sent me to a boarding school."

"You have any siblings?"

"Yes, a younger brother."

"Where is he staying?"

"He's still young to understand the problem. So he's staying with my mom."

"I'm sorry Ashish."

"No, don't be Surya. It's no problem. I must study hard and make them proud. At least from the marks I get, they should be happy and forget the fight."

"Don't worry Ashish. Sure they will be free and from eleventh grade you will stay with your parents."

"Thank you Surya, now come on let us go for the games hour."

"No, perhaps today I will stay in the dorm. I'll come for the study hour directly."

"Okay, bye Surya. Dhanush has called me for a basketball match."

"Bye!"

Ashish went. Surya though felt relieved when he spoke with Ashish, diverting his mind, was now sad again. His family's thoughts never went from his mind. His sorrow went to the peak when he saw his wrist. He wore his dad's watch. Surya's hand resembled his dad's. He saw his dad's arm. He wanted to touch his dad's arm. Hold his fingers tightly. Feel its warmth. But all he had was nothing but the watch. It was then... Surya felt the horror of homesickness. No one could ever escape from this sorrow. This sad feeling, no one can console. This feeling had no remedy in A.K.R.S. Not even the greatest, most talented doctors can cure this. This was such a bad feeling, only those who felt it can understand. The watch was curing the sickness and was also increasing it. Surya cried and cried throughout the games hour. No one was there to wipe off his tears.

By 6:30, it was study hour. All the students who went to play came back. Ashish too had come now.

"Are you still crying?"

"Yes, I cannot tolerate this feeling."

"It's good"

"What?"

"Crying" Surya frowned. He didn't know what Ashish meant. Ashish continued.

"The only thing you should do to take away your homesickness is cry. Even I did the same. It will be like this for a month. Later it'll all be right. Now come on its study hour. You can't stay here now. Go wash your face and come. I'll wait."

All of them walked to their classrooms. The classes they were studying were their study hour classrooms too. Surya couldn't concentrate on the studies. Moreover, it was the first day in school. No lessons were taught. He was free, he felt lonely. He saw the students near him. All were talking, joking, playing tricks, in simple had fun. Surya was also the guy who did all these in free periods. The study hour was also a free period now but Surya could not feel the same happiness. Whatever he did to divert his mind, he couldn't get out of the sadness. He consoled himself often "everything will be okay." But how long can he console? It's up to his heart. The study hour was over by 8:45 then it was dinnertime. Surya could not eat well. His stomach never felt hunger. His stomach never felt a satisfactory diet that was first available with mother's love. Later, after dinner, Surya and Ashish had some chat and went to bed. There ending his first day in A.K.R.S.

Chapter 4: Coming Home

*D*ays in A.K.R.S. went in the same way. It has been 26 days that Surya has joined A.K.R.S. It was no different than the first day. Each and every day, Surya's sadness increased. He cannot escape from it. He stopped listening, he forgot how to smile. Whenever he sees himself in the mirror, some thought would make him feel trapped. The hostel phone never rang for him. He did not get even one call. He was broke. Every day, he'd stand by the phone and wait for his parents to call. He'd sometimes tell the parents of other children to call his parents and tell them that he's waiting for the phone. But nothing has ever come for him.

One day, when he was waiting for the phone, he saw a wonder. A play station portable; in short, PSP. It's a gaming device. Surya was attracted on seeing it. A tenth grader was playing with it. Surya's most big entertainment was video games. He forgot that he was waiting for the call, and was curiously watching what was in the game. But when the student went out, it was then he had realised he was waiting for the phone. He never told any parents to call either. He felt ashamed. He forgot his duty. But to Surya, he is a boy who loves stuffs like video games, bikes, art. Whatever he's doing, if any of these three come by; he'll lose his mind in them. Everyone has their choice of interest. Surya is dipped in these stuffs.

That night Surya couldn't sleep. He was scolding himself for not staying by the phone. He cursed, scolded and even slapped himself for it. This thing what Surya does, is the reason why he's unstable. He has a clash between his mind and heart all the time. Each and every time, his heart would search for a desire, stays in it, and enjoys it. Once done, only then his mind comes to play. It'll scold the heart with no mercy. This will happen a lot of time in Surya's life. He does a thing with joy, and then he feels sad about it. This demon character of Surya never let him enjoy anything completely.

Now, let us get back to the story. His mind after all the hardships faced, rested by 11:00 pm. The next day was Friday, the last working day of the week. Remember what Surya said about the Parent's visit, during each and every weekends? The school didn't allow any one. Only when a child gets an out pass, even the parents were allowed. Surya didn't know that. He thought there might be some problem at home. This increased his sadness; this was the typical mind set of Surya in A.K.R.S. whatever he did. He gets reminded of his family, then again he feels sad. His friends started avoiding him. They are not happy with a friend who always cries. So they never actually called Surya for anything. This went on and on and on.

One day, after dinner, Surya went to his bed after eating the dreadful dinner and went to bed straight away. Then there came a seventh-grader calling Surya.

"Who is Surya? Is he here? He got a call from his parents."

Surya jumped from his bed. He didn't even land his foot properly in ground. He was actually flying, his heart too. He ran as fast as possible and reached to the telephone and said…

"Hello?"

"Hello? Surya It's me, daddy!" His dad said.

Surya burst into tears on hearing this. He cried over the phone. It was this, what he was expecting all these 26 long days. Though it was just days, he felt it as 26 long years. His feelings were a mixture of uncontrollable happiness, sadness, fulfilment, satisfaction, anger and longing. All these feelings gave him the power to cry, but not to speak.

"Surya, You there?" said his father again.

After a moment Surya tried to control himself and said,

"Yes dad. Why didn't anyone call me? It's been 26 days! You know, I waited by the phone for these many days. Are you so busy that you forgot me? Do you know what is happening here? Don't you even have time to call me? Okay you're busy, what is with mom? Don't you all even worry that I'm somewhere here? Did you leave all your love and affection after you imprisoned me? Can't you even call the first day? Listen to me speaking about how the first day at school was? Or did you think I would forget you all after leaving me here? 26 days dad… 26 full days… you… won't… know how… I… missed you all… "Surya gasped for breath. To be precise he can't speak anymore. His cry has stopped his strength to speak. All he did was cry louder by

the phone. He couldn't even hear the sound of his dad's shock yelling "Hello? Surya? Hello? Talk to me Surya??

Surya continued, "Dad, please dad, take me home... I don't want this school dad... I don't want it... its hell here daddy... my heart is so heavy right now... I couldn't bear the pain dad... it's too painful dad... please come and get me dad... I'm powerless against this dad. I couldn't tolerate..."

His dad had an opportunity at least now. He spoke to Surya "Surya! Surya! Please listen to me. Just be calm Surya. Surya, work is not even a size of an ant when it comes to you. Is this all you've ever known about my love to you? Our family's love to you?"

"Then why haven't you called?" asked Surya struggling to talk in his continuous cry.

"Surya, we have tried each and every second we had, all these days! If you come here, you'll see my nokia-n73's button damaged just because of all the calls I've made you! But each and every time I never get it connected. Your hostel's phone is engaged every time I try." Surya's dad explained.

This was a dreadful problem in A.K.R.S. the hostel had only one phone, with 467 students' parents to call. So, it really needs luck to get a chance to speak. The ratio would be 1:467. Both Surya and his dad didn't know that, for Surya waited for the call and his dad desperately trying continuously for it. Without knowing all this Surya's dad continued speaking.

"Ask mom too Surya. She is too upset. We couldn't tolerate your absence in this house. Wherever we see, we miss your presence all around this house." Surya's dad started crying.

"Dad, please daddy, get me out of this place! This is hell! I cannot explain it in words! But I'm burning here! That's all I can say! My whole self! My brain, my legs, my hands, my eyes, my total soul, they are burning dad!" Surya had a pause, gasping for breath in his tears as he continued, "please dad, let me leave this dreadful place! I don't care if it takes a year for me to change school! I just don't want to be here anymore! Please dad! PLEASE!!!!"

"Surya, I and your mother have planned the same Surya! I've already spoke to the president of C.B.W. School and he said re-admission can be granted! That's why I've tried more than before to call you today! I'll tell the details later! We'll be seeing you this Saturday Surya! This Saturday you will be in our home! I'll tell everything later! Now bye Surya! I'm having a bad reception here. I'll tell everything on the way back Surya in person. Good bye Surya!"

"Ok goodbye dad!" Surya said, wiping off his tears.

"Good night, my son! Sleep peacefully"

That was the day... after so much hardships, Surya felt a feeling, the feeling that he was about to forget, the feeling which he carried at almost all of the time till his eighth grade, the feeling that conquers him whenever he gets whatever he wants, the feeling that he got before *the Alice in the wonderland tragedy, What was that feeling? Well, Surya was feeling Happiness.*

He was convinced that he's about to escape his fate. He's about to see his mom's face after school, hear his dad's voice, play with his brother, see his old friends, have a good walk from school to what he could happily call, 'Home'.

With this happiness, Surya was thinking about his school. His best buddies in C.B.W. Krishna, Raymond and all the people of his Eighth grade whom he had grown up with. With all these thoughts playing in his head, a sudden beam of light fell in his heart.

Going back to C.B.W. had a more good reason now. A sudden explosion of happiness inside his heart, the extreme pulse a boy can get, the feeling that can even make big warriors collapse to their feet, making them weak and strong at the same time. Chilling the soul, soothing the heat in the brain, finding a soft melody that could ring forever in the heart... a feeling that no one in this world could fight back... called Love...

Chapter 5: The Lab incident.

A thought struck Surya, Going back to his old school, means he's about to see his love, he's going to meet her again, fate has finally paid him, he is about to go and fall into her sight. He is going to meet Shivani again...

On thinking of the name Shivani, Surya felt a breeze gently caressing his hair, running its hand over Surya's long face. He felt a thunder bolt in his heart that he forgot all his worries in a matter of a nanosecond. He was carried away, with the feelings of his first meeting with Shivani.

It was celebration time for C.B.W.; Students were singing, dancing, acting, laughing and playing. Why? Because it is cultural fest for C.B.W. all the classes were decorated with colour papers, balloons, boards with drawings of celebration indicating that the cultural fest is around the corner, in the next week. School was not school anymore. The sound of angry teachers was converted to a beautiful million birds chirping, sounds of happy students were not only heard, but felt everywhere in the school premises. Each and every student was engaged in the cultural.

It's the physics lab, the gigantic lab filled with toys that teaches physics. A strict attender whose harsh voice to protect those instruments had stopped coming for two weeks now. Why? It's because students are now preparing their song performance in the lab. The Song was "Heal the

*world" by Michael Jackson. All the tuning fork didn't echo the 'hum',
but it echoed the beautiful melody sung by these children.*

*It was a group of 33 comprising 13 boys and 20 girls. The co-
ordinator for this performance was Surya's English teacher Mrs Shelly.
On seeing the performance in the perspective of the audience, she felt
arranging the students and making them sing was not enough to give
a colourful performance. So she decided make a small scene that has
to be played by two children; a boy who is dressed evil, who takes
mother earth in his hands and plays with it carelessly, indicating the
trouble we are giving to mother earth, fighting wars, genocide, and
all the unhappy doings a man commits. And the other one was a girl.
An angel, who restores peace, retrieves the earth from the demon and
heals it with love and care. It would look like a skit that explains the
lyrics, is what she thought of.*

*Mrs Shelly found the boy. But they were in search of the girl. The
ma'am had asked the girls in the group whether they have anyone
in their mind, for the role to be played as the angel. Shruti, a name
Surya would never forget, Told She knows one. Accepting that she
knows a girl who is beautiful, pretty, and who can act very well, as
per the conditions of the ma'am, got out of the lab. She returned in
a few minutes, announcing that she had come. Surya who till now
never took place in the decision making process, now wanted to see
the girl who was described, "Beautiful and pretty". He had a thought
that none of the girls in C.B.W. was pretty. He was about to tease
Shruti that "you call 'this' pretty, Shruti? You definitely don't have*

eyes as well as taste." While these thoughts were flowing in his mind, Shivani entered.

Shivani was in eighth grade too. She had an Indian white complexion. Her hair was cut till the shoulders which was straight from the top and curled slightly at the end, it bounced lovely syncing her walks, through which a golden glittered ear-ring was swaying front and back, her eyes were big and cute that were remarkably artistic like a still water lighted by a full moon. She was not too tall or short. She was just the way an eighth grade girl should be. She was as tender as a just bloomed rose on a snowy fresh morning. Surya, though was off the earth noticed all of them.

Surya was dumb-struck and was instantly swept off his feet on Shivani's beauty. She was a girl that Surya never even dreamt of; she was a girl he never thought about, she was a girl Surya didn't even know exists in real life, altogether it was a pleasurable and the most intense shock as well as surprise he had experienced till now. It was as if the most hand-picked angels' queen had come to earth to take away Surya from this place. No words could ever make a distant equality for a beauty that Shivani carried through the doors of the physics lab. She was a man's Goddess, and a woman's pure carrier of ego.

"She indeed is an Angel!" Said Surya, mesmerised on his angel.

"What?" Shelly ma'am asked.

Surya, who got back to Earth by the question the ma'am asked, just realised that he spoke it out what he thought of Shivani being an angel.

"*She would really suit the character, is what I was supposing to tell ma'am.*" Surya said, escaping from the situation.

The faculty was explaining what the programme was about, what role the angel had, to Shivani. She told she'd accept the role.

The ma'am had told Shivani to watch the song for the first time to see the performance then rehearse it with her the next time. She had made all the students stand to their positions and perform it to Shivani... Surya loved to stand in front and represent himself to Shivani. The song began... Shivani was randomly seeing the performance. She saw the children's actions and smile while they were singing. She had a quick glance at each of the people there. She gave the same time interval for Surya too. But that was more than enough for our boy... Surya saw Shivani eye to eye. She saw him at the edge of her eyes. He noticed that, he saw it sparkled to the light around. Her big, round and poetic eyes, Saw him. It was as if the reflections were fire from guns of magic sparkles that attacked right through Surya's heart. Surya can't control his body. It was as excited as a race car that was waiting for the wave of the flag, to start a race.

As the song was finished, Surya couldn't wait. He was so much active. He asked permission from Shelly ma'am to go out for a drink of water, where he just ran out of the lab and was running around the whole school, to calm down his hyper-excited soul. The whole day, he was as happy as the lab incident, where his mind was fully occupied with the angel's eyes...

Chapter 6: C.B.W. Again.

*T*he lab incident planted a smile on Surya's face. It has been days since he smiled. It's a fresh memory of joy that Surya had cherished. He loved the weightlessness he had in his heart. It literally made him feel lighter. The problems Surya had, has been solved. It was not a matter of days that he's going to get out of the hell he willingly got into.

Surya, though happy was suddenly wondering. 'Why did this dreadful place looked so much heavenly when I saw it first? I was aware that I would be leaving my parents. Yet, it had turned into a sudden and intense pain on being here.' Well Surya didn't have an answer; as it was with his fate's designer, someone Godly.

The weekend came. His mom and dad had arrived to the school office, having shown a medical certificate about Surya's childhood problem, faking a reason to take transfer from A.K.R.S. The warden on Surya's dormitory saw it strange that Surya had been packing it all night. Whereas, his parents had just now informed on taking him back.

All is set and off went the Maruti 800 out of the A.K.R.S. This time the car didn't have the mixed feelings inside it when they had come for admission in A.K.R.S. All it had was Joy in each and every corner of the small car, and off it went to Surya's hometown.

31

'Bye, ma!' said Surya. His voice had been the clearest, happiest on the last few days. It has been 11days after Surya was brought out of A.K.R.S. He had now prepared ready with his black Hercules Turbo-drive, to go back to C.B.W. His days of happiness are back. The stolen piece of his life is back to its place.

He locked his cycle on the edge of the cycle park, sentimentally his cycle's position from his fifth grade. He marched on happily, like a king returning from a battle victoriously. Surya had happiness in the face, sense of belongingness in the mind, eager to see his beloved friends in the heart.

The class of 9th D was so surprised and happy for the return of their friend, for all they shouted 'Surya!' as he stepped inside. Surya was *so flattered by the love of his friends. It's indeed a home-coming for Surya for he was back to his home, his C.B.W.*

As the day went by, Surya had enormous chats with his friends, he was introduced to each and every teacher by his friends, and he still had his English ma'am from seventh grade. He after a long time ate the samosas that were sold at the break time. Saw all his teachers and was explaining why he had come back. He never listened to the classes on his first day; he was speaking with his friends, Raymond and Krishna the whole time. They were mostly chatting about the newly admitted members in the class.

At the noon, Surya went to his home for lunch. Happily saying the day's progress to his mom; Satisfied with the lunch served deliciously with love. He ate it full. He was stuffed. Later he took the books for the second half of the day, and again went to school. The day went well. But Surya wanted to see Shivani. There was only one place to find her, the van stand.

There were a bunch of private vans that were assigned to help children reach their homes, by the children's parents. Shivani belongs to a place which is not in the township Surya was in. She lives for nearly 20 kilometres away. So she was assigned to a van too. Surya had seen her go by the van. He eagerly went early so that he could make an appearance for her after a very long time. He was unsure that Shivani could remember him. He saw and fell in love with Shivani, but he never spoke to her. Yet, with full of eagerness, he waited in the van stand.

'She'd never remember you.' said Pravin. Pravin was Surya's classmate and both were friends. They both sit together in the class. Pravin was aware of Surya's love towards Shivani. Nearly the whole class knew. It was when Surya had told Krishna about Shivani, Krishna's mouth got something to chew upon for the entire class. Krishna loved revealing all the secrets his friends share with him. He, on hearing the topic, really found a good role in spreading the news.

'I know, let's see.' replied Surya.

Shivani came through the gate. Surya was happy to see the angel. She had grown a little. She wasn't the small pretty cute girl Surya saw in the lab. Yet, she was still beautiful. Her eyes, the poetic eyes, though were tired from the whole day learning at school, remained poetic. It never lost its beauty even after these nine months. She was still an angel. Surya was seeing all of this. He felt the same breeze that caressed him, whenever he thought of Shivani. His heart was pounding to speak with her, while there was also a little fear in doing it.

Whether it was God's design or merely a co-incidence, Shivani caught Surya seeing her. He just turned away, as everyone does. He was so excited, yet afraid and later decided to leave the van stand. But he later decided to stay, for he desperately missed Shivani. Moreover, Krishna hasn't come yet; he had to wait for him anyway. Surya was seeing Shivani the whole time and whenever she turned, he'd look away. This happened for nearly fifteen minutes. Later as Shivani's van was about to depart, Surya again peeped at her. She was standing in the doorstep of the van. It was usually the place Shivani had always stood. She saw him again. But this time, Surya never turned.

He deliberately wanted Shivani to see him, seeing her. Both of them, from their respective places, didn't show any expressions but they just saw, as blank as a white paper. Shivani showed a faint smile in seeing him, Surya was so happy on seeing her smiling at him. His heart started pumping fast. The juices of love, happiness, satisfaction was flowing all over his valves and chambers of his heart. It was this sight that he had to see, after coming back from a month of sadness. He had a happiness that an abandoned sailor would have, on seeing a land after a lone struggle at the ocean. It lured all of his senses, he was physically standing in the ground, but his heart ran, rolled and floated around the slowly departing van.

He was even more surprised for Shivani broadening her smile at him. He never expected this to happen. He had known that the whole school knows about his feelings for Shivani, thanks to Krishna for that. So eventually Shivani would have known that too and yet, she smiles at him! This led to a conclusion to Surya.

'I think she likes me!' mumbled Surya. The thought had struck to him clearly. The girl knew the fact that he loves her, yet if she smiles at him, it had just one answer. It's that, she likes him too!

'What?' Pravin asked Surya.

'She likes me! ... She likes me! ... SHE LIKES ME!!' shouted Surya, lifting up Pravin to express his happiness. Pravin, equally confused for what had happen, was shouting on Surya to put him down.

While all this happened, Krishna had come through the gate. Surya on seeing Krishna instantly dropped Pravin and warned him to keep this as a secret. Surya had experienced Krishna's wrath once; of course it had turned out well now. Anyway, he thought this must be a secret for Krishna. Both the friends bid bye to Pravin as his van was about to depart now, and started walking to home.

'How was A.K.R.S. Surya?' asked Krishna. He was Surya's best friend. They were nearly neighbours for Krishna lived in the adjacent street from Surya's house. The two boys were walking to home, through the evening sun that produced a bright orange environment, which was going through the twilight.

'It had pretty cool infrastructure but I never liked it. I missed my family so much.'

'Oh stop it.! I never asked about the buildings!'

'You never change, do you? Your best buddy had suffered out there, for nearly a month and yet you're asking this.' Teased Surya, for what he had understood Krishna's question was not about the school, but the girls in it.

'Oh, people change after drastic circumstances or due to a small jealousy. Dude, I haven't undergone through any of this till now.'

'Well I've changed a bit.'

'Yeah, you're smile has changed a lot. You were a guy that had a carefree smile always. But the damn school had made it disappear from my friend's face.'

'Ha-ha! Since when did you develop a care on me?'

'I had always cared for you my friend. It's a pity that you haven't noticed yet.'

'Oh! Yeah! I remember your care; you're the one who advertised the whole school about my feelings for Shivani. That's really caring indeed.'

'You should thank me for that man! It's a friend's duty to spread the news of love! And it also worked out good; Shivani once came to me and asked about you! But sad that you weren't there.'

'What…! She asked about me???'

'Yes! It was the other day that I and…' Krishna started telling a beautiful tale that had come in nearly thousands of movies where the heroine had asked for a hero. Surya though understood that this was his friend's standard lies that he'd always come up to startle Surya for a moment. Surya didn't want his friend's party to be crashed. He just gave the reactions that would encourage his story better. Surya really missed all of this, for the poor boy went to A.K.R.S.

After that, it was half past four; Surya reached the road that reached to his home. It was then Krishna had said, 'Are you interested in badminton Surya?'

'I was actually, me, Shruti, Balu and Nisha had played it in the streets in childhood. But I don't know if it interests me yet.'

'Oh, shut up! Come to PC by five o'clock Surya! Bye!' ordered a leaving Krishna. It was his style to make his friends do a work. He never cared for the otherwise either.

'Okay, I'll try.' Replied Surya, and the two friends walked their ways.

Chapter 7: Badminton.

*S*urya had gone to PC, the Palar Club. It's a place where recreational activities like indoor games, a gym, and a lovely open theatre had been constructed. People doesn't have to pay money for it as it was in control of the company Surya's dad had been working. Surya was first scared of that place. A most dreadful incident had happened to Surya in the very same place.

It was when Surya was seven years old. He had participated in a singing competition the club had arranged for a dinner evening. Surya from the beginning was so excited to participate in it. Only God knows why he come up with something called singing. Maybe it was a way Surya thought of representing himself in a crowd or maybe he just wanted to test his luck in singing or he just wanted to sing! Well, God knows the answer.

Well, he sure practiced a lot. But what Surya did was that, he chose a female solo as his song. He had no choice for little Surya's voice was still soft and childish. Surya chose it, practiced it, and was so happy to even sing it. But the fun started on reaching the place, and seeing the judge.

The judge's stare completely paralysed Surya. Surya always had a fear for skinny old people. He always wanted to avoid them; it had given him goose bumps on seeing the judge, a tall skinny bald man, with so much white hair in his face. The judge even had added a good spice. He was literally staring at Surya, as if his glasses were to be poked by the very eyes in it. Surya on seeing this didn't even greet the audience. Well, he didn't even sing too; He just read out the lyrics he knew and ran away crying loudly.

This happened when Surya was a child. But a teen Surya, considered it as a great shame. Well, coming out from the dreadful lawn, he stepped into the badminton hall which was right beside it. That was the place Surya would define heaven. That is going to be the place, where he's going to meet his talents warmly welcoming him.

The badminton court was not yet occupied for the day. Surya was the first to enter it. It was dark as there were no lights lit up. Of course, it was 6:00 p.m. There couldn't be any sunlight left to light it naturally. So Surya searched for the switch for the lights and had switched it on when he found one. At once the whole court was lit up. It was then

Surya found how big the court was, and how well it was made up with wood. He was shocked to see such a big court for the badminton game. He played it only in the streets before. He never knew any rules in badminton. All he knew was, if the cork had come to him, he should beat it with a racquet. So, for a boy of that knowledge, he found the normal sized court really gigantic. He walked through the sides for few minutes. He was really confused whether he could even shoot cork from end to end.

After all this, Surya sat on a chair nearby. He was waiting for Krishna to come. In a few minutes, Surya saw Krishna come, through the window of the court room. But with him, Surya also saw many girls who were accompanying Krishna. One short girl, with fair complexion, the other was a little taller when compared to the former, with a little more fairer complexion as well, and then there was also a girl with an average height. Surya also saw two medium dark girls where one was short and the other one tall. While Surya was shocked to see five girls coming with Krishna, He also noticed another tall dark guy coming with him. Surya never saw these people with Krishna before. He also knew the fact that they too, would be friends with him soon. So he waited in anxiety to get introduced to them.

Krishna opened the doors of the court hard; they went swinging and slammed into the walls that supported them. Later every one entered, and saw Surya with curiosity of who he is.

"Hey! Surya! I never expected you to come!" Said a Surprised Krishna!

"*You ordered me to come remember?*" *said Surya.*

"*Oh, I see*" *said Krishna, with a notorious Smile. Later he continued to introduce the people who were nearby.*

"*Hey Surya, let me introduce these people to you! See this short fly? Her name is Preethi. She is in sixth grade.*" *pointing towards the shortest girl, said Krishna.*

"*…and this is Akansha, and Divya, both of them in seventh grades.*" *pointing to the fairer, short and tall girls respectively, Continued Krishna.*

"*…finally this is Neha and Dhanvita.*" *Pointing to the medium dark girls, shorter and taller respectively, said Krishna.*

"*Hey people. I'm Surya.*"

"*Hi!*" *the whole gang in the place said in chorus.*

"*Hey bro, I'm Varun. I'm in tenth.*" *The tall guy introduced himself.*

"*Hey man!*" *by saying this, Surya gave a high five to Varun. He was somehow immediately was comfy with Varun.*

"*Do you play Shuttle too, Surya?*" *Preethi asked.*

"*Well, I thought I could play a little, but on seeing the court and all your racquet covers, I'm sure I really don't know anything about this.*" *After seeing all their big bags for the racquets, Surya answered Preethi.*

"*Which grade are you Surya?*" *Akansha questioned.*

"9th"

"Do you know, Swati? She's 9th too. She's my friend." Divya asked.

"Would you stop it? Swati isn't any movie star So that everyone knows her!" Neha interrupted Divya as she knew that this was a dumb question that Divya is making.

"Well, Divya, first, I don't know Swati, I'm sorry for that, and Neha, why are you angry at Swati?" riddled Surya.

"She's not that worth her anger." Dhanvita started speaking.

"Well, all of you seem to have an unfinished business with whoever that Swati is. All I have to do is to pray for that poor soul who'd suffer your wrath." Said Surya, kidding.

"Phew, is it over? Do you people remember that we've come to play Shuttle?" said Krishna, as he was too bored on the talks.

"Okay man, come on! Come in Surya!" Varun invited Surya as he went inside the court.

"Don't you have your racquet umm…"asked Surya to Dhanvita.

"…Dhanvita."

"Yeah. Sorry. Don't you play Badminton Dhanvita?"

"No."

"Why?"

"I don't like it."

"Then why are you coming?"

"I come for my friends."

"Isn't it boring? To just sit and see?"

"Why are you Speaking too much?!"

"Well, you aren't that's why."

"I don't like unnecessary talks." Saying this, Dhanvita turned away. She wanted to stop the conversation.

Surya didn't like Dhanvita. She was so stern, and rude. Dhanvita would always like to speak with only the people she likes. She would give more preference to the looks about whom she's speaking than their characters. Our Surya really doesn't have that capturing physique. As we already know that he's a little obese for an average guy in that age. So there's no way of becoming a good friend with Dhanvita. Actually it's really a miracle for her being still friendly to the other girls present in the shuttle court as well. Surya too, didn't care for a good friendship with Dhanvita. His approach with people was completely opposite to hers. As Surya never care for looks, but he'd surely love a person based on their character.

"Hey guys, can anyone teach me badminton?" Surya shouted as if he was announcing it.

"You sit down and watch us play. We'll teach you as we play."

Surya sat straight opposite to the place where Dhanvita was sitting. Both of them were beside the net that runs through the centre of the court. As Surya watched Varun, Krishna, Neha and Divya play.

Krishna had started the match with his serve. While Divya countered, by hitting the cork higher. Then suddenly Surya saw Varun running in and strongly hit a smash. To which Neha's shortness helped in taking it at ease and passing it to the opposite court. Surya saw this with great awe. Most of the times, he never saw the cork, but he could see all of them acting as if they predicted the cork's path.

Surya just realized that either, he had to quit, or he has a long way to go in this game. Then he saw Dhanvita. If he quits, he'd become more like Dhanvita. Just sitting there and watching the game. Surya instantly left over the thought of quitting it. He after the very same match, wanted to go inside and play. So he borrowed Krishna's racquet and teamed up with Varun and started playing. To Surya's surprise, he felt no discomfort in playing such a new game. His doubt of shooting the cork from end to end happened. Sometimes it went beyond that too. He felt the court's actual size soon. Later he had a good confidence in him becoming a badminton player.

After alternate turns on playing. All the people in the court except Dhanvita were exhausted. They decided to leave. They started packing up their stuffs to go home.

"You're too good for a beginner Surya!" said Divya.

"Thanks. Even I'm surprised with that fact, Div." Surya replied.

"Will you come tomorrow too?" Akansha asked Surya.

"Why wouldn't I? This is the coolest place I've seen till now."

"So he doesn't like it because of us. It's just the court." Krishna teased.

"Ha-ha... good one bro. Well as a matter of fact, I love this place especially because of you guys."

"Are we done with all these dumb dialogues?" Dhanvita said in a tired voice, indicating her irritations of the speech.

"Yes, Grumpy Goat." said Surya.

Everyone started laughing on hearing Surya call Dhanvita as 'Grumpy Goat'. They knew that she deserved it and they sometimes wanted to tease her as well for her behaviour but on seeing her friendship they decided not to. Surya on other hand didn't care anything about her and called her so. Dhanvita was so shocked and embarrassed, couldn't hold her temper.

"Shut up! You stupid fat donkey" Dhanvita shouted at Surya and stormed out of the court and started walking away fast from the badminton court.

"Oh my God, Hey, I just teased for fun guys, she could've teased me again. Can I go tell her sorry?" asked Surya, startled on Dhanvita's reaction.

"Oh no leave it Surya. She'll be alright. We'll convince her. Don't worry. We'll see you tomorrow. Bye!" said Preethi.

"Bye Surya!" Said the others to Surya and Krishna, who were about to depart together to their homes too.

"Do you think she'd forgive me?" Surya asked Krishna. Still upset about the incident that happened few minutes ago.

"Don't worry about it man! She's always like this. She'd only speak if people are looking good and who behave like millionaires."

"What dumb logic is that?"

"It's the way she'd think they're equal to her!"

"Then how the hell do you manage Krish? Ha-ha!"

"It really is a head-ache dude!"

Both the friends gave a slight laugh and started speaking about other things on their way back to home. Surya had a fresh mood that day till sleep. It was as if one day at play had made him healthier as a horse. He was really active. He had said to himself that he must go for the game each and every possible day, and also he had to maintain a distance with Dhanvita. With all those thoughts lingering, Surya rested his head in the pillow, and went to sleep by 12:39 a.m.

Chapter 8: What's the worst that can happen?

"*Excuse me ma'am!*" *Shivani came in after asking permission from Mrs Shelly, the English teacher in the class of 9th D.*

"*Ah! Shivani! Come in!*" *Mrs Shelly welcomed Shivani.*

"*Dude, Shivani!!!!!*" *exclaimed a shocked Krishna, to Surya who was reading the phrases of the lesson loudly to the class. It's the lessons about the Bermuda Triangle. Surya had a loud and clear voice, which always had given him an opportunity, to read out the lesson to the whole class sentence by sentence for the teacher to explain it at regular intervals. This was also one such day, where Surya was reading an essay of the Bermuda Triangle, where very large ships and airplanes have been sunk deep into the ocean due to the 'mysterious forces' at the North Atlantic Ocean. Now it is time, for Surya's ship to sink into Shivani's 'mysterious forces'.*

Surya suddenly stopped reading and looked at Shivani. He now experienced the same vacuum in his heart, that he had on the lab incident; A vacuum, which would suck in all of universe's happiness to one small chamber. He now saw that she was speaking to ma'am for an announcement to make to the whole class, while the English teacher had questioned about the announcement's details. After a few talks Shivani had turned to the crowd and saw Surya standing. She gave a puzzled look at the boy standing and reading before. Surya too, was puzzled that time, because he didn't know why Shivani is seeing him like that now. Shivani had smiled at Surya by the van stand the other day. All of a sudden now she's giving a strange look at Surya. Surya didn't know what to do, but he still gave a blank look at Shivani.

"Oh, you continue dear" Said Mrs Shelly to Shivani and continued,

"Sit down Surya, Students! Listen to the announcement this girl is about to give."

Acquiring the signal from the teacher, Shivani started speaking. This is the first time Surya was about hear Shivani's voice. Actually, throughout the 'Heal the World' performance, Surya never spoke to Shivani. He always watched her from a distance; she too rarely spoke with the girls present there. So, Surya 'braced' himself to hear the voice of his Shivani.

"The Managements of the Schools in our district and Chennai have organised a cultural and extra-curricular contest in the inter-school level, to which 31 schools have been selected to participate. Our school too, is one of them. There are several events that are organised in various categories in the primary, senior and super-senior levels. Interested students are requested to participate in the auditions held at Gandhi Hall after 3:50. Further details about the categories and eligibility would be informed there. Thank you."

After finishing the announcement, Shivani immediately said Thank you to Mrs Shelly and at once left the place. Surya was motion-less, speech-less, expression-less, on the shock Shivani's voice produced in him. Her voice was sweet, a good, feminine, soft and humble voice. It's not a voice that can sing; it's not every man's mesmerizing voice; it's not a voice that can lift you up into paradise! It's a normal voice for a teenage girl. Well for Surya, it was his Shivani's voice, which lifted him up.

"I'm going to go for it, Krishna!" Surya said to Krishna, whispering.

"Are you out of your Goddamn mind? Didn't you hear? Where you going by your stupid, vacuum thunderbolts thing again? It's a cultural cum extra-curricular competition Surya! Neither of us knows..." Krishna was interrupted by the teacher's words telling Surya to continue his recital.

"Why are you so late? You took only half a minute in every other classes!" a girl asked Shivani.

"Oh, I'm sorry! It's just that... I forgot... I forgot what to tell for a moment!"

"You forgot?!" The girl again asked, shocked from Shivani's reply.

"Yeah, I just didn't know... how to start the announcement! I couldn't speak for a while... plus, Shelly ma'am asked me about the event personally at first. So I had to announce it two times. Sorry!" Shivani replied to the girl, who was first waiting outside the class.

"*Are you afraid of Shelly ma'am? You know that she's the only kind teacher all of C.B.W.! Why were you startled on saying it to her!?*" asked the girl, confused on Shivani's behaviour.

"*Oh! I wasn't startled when I was saying that to ma'am, my dear friend!*"

"*Well… then?*"

"*Remember that I told you about a boy who was staring at me by the van stand that day?*"

"*Yes?*"

"*I saw him! He's of this class!*"

"*Well?*"

"*I couldn't speak when I saw him!*"

"*What!?*"

"*Yes! He was doing his recital of the lesson. So he was standing up straight. I saw him. Somehow, I forgot what I had to say!*"

"*Why?*"

"*Ughh! Will you stop asking these one word questions! Seriously, it's difficult to answer! You won't understand anything!*"

"*Right, First I'll see this guy who's reciting!*" Saying this, the girl looked at the window of 9th D. She couldn't see anyone standing up! All were seated.

"There's no one reciting Shiv!"

"Look clearly you blind duck!" Shivani teased.

"Oh I am seeing girl! No one's reciting!" the girl said.

"What?"

"All I see is the guy I hate the most the world." The girl said, explaining her anger!

"Yea? Who's that?" Shivani asked.

"The one who teased me at the club, remember?"

"Oh! Yea! Who's it? Show me!" Shivani tried to peep in and see who that boy was. Suddenly,

"Is there a problem girls?" Shelly ma'am asked the two girls. She had come out of the class after the few lines Surya had recited.

"No ma'am not at all!" replied the girl; in a sudden recovery from the shock shelly ma'am had placed.

"Then you have to be leaving I suppose? Don't you have any classes?"

"Yes ma'am! Right away!" Shivani quickly got into motion on saying this.

After a few steps from 9th D, Shivani and the other girl was relieved to have escaped. They had been standing at the door of 8th A.

"I couldn't see him!" Shivani said, panting.

"He's not worth it! Leave it Shiv." The girl replied.

"*Don't be angry on him! He might be a good boy. He might have said for fun! Take it easy girl!*" Shivani was trying to console the other girl.

"*With a look like that, he's making fun of me? He'd die if he ever speaks with me like that again!*" The girl burst out in anger!

"*Look! Control your temper first and relax. See you tomorrow!*" Shivani said.

"*Okay then! Bye Shiv!*"

"*Good bye Dhanvita!*"

Chapter 9: Vaibhav: Cultural competition

"No, no, no, no, no, no, no! This is a bad idea!" Krishna said to Surya. Krishna was clearly explaining Surya about his fear for cultural participations.

"Leave your fear you!? It's the only way I can get close to Shivani. Don't you see?"

"You fool! If you want to get to Shivani you go and suicide! Why are you calling me to accompany you?"

"Come on Krishna! Now don't cry, just do what I do!"

"Dude! From day one since my birth I resisted all this cultural thingies like dance, music, drama... oi... they had always given me goose bumps and shivers in stage!"

"Anyway, you're not going to go to the main stage unless you qualify!"

"That's obvious of course!"

"Then what's the problem! Come with me! Anyway you won't qualify then why worry facing the stage?"

"Anyway I won't qualify, then why are you 'calling me' worrying me! Leave me ALONE!"

Surya watched Krishna escape from Surya's grip and running furiously with his school bag swaying from left to right. Surya couldn't even imagine that the 'mighty' Krishna was afraid of the stage! It was this very same Krishna who'd play and win 'nearly-lost' soccer and badminton matches so heroic, that he would provide the effect of Sylvester Stallone's Rambo movie climax. Well, everyone have weaknesses, don't they?

After Surya's recovery from the shock Krishna provided, Surya had to go in alone for the audition camp. The place was so crowded with a sound that no teacher had stopped shouting at; even teachers were a part of it! Surya watched throughout the hall.

"It would've been a massacre to Krishna!"

Surya laughed within him and started searching for Shivani. His main aim was to search for her, ask her to help into getting in for few auditions in this crowd, and do those auditions successfully and return back as a friend to Shivani. Also, if he had found Shivani in any of the auditions he'd try hard to get selected to it and be going for the competitions with her. He really loved the second one and was praying for it to happen. His plan was well drafted, but the small drawback in its execution is, God had planned something else for Surya.

"Surya!?" Surya heard someone calling his name feebly. He turned towards the direction it came from. It was by the English skit side. He saw Varun coming to him.

"Varun! You're here? Finally I've got a company for me!" Surya said in a tone of relief.

"I'm not just a company man! I'm on a work here!" Varun said.

"What would it be?"

"Look, I've got selected to the English skit competition. Our story impressed the teacher and he wanted us to do it directly at Vaibhav!"

"Oh, really?" That's awesome man!"

"Well, actually, I've got a problem now." Varun said in a serious tone.

"What's that?"

"I've got all the artists. Except…"

"Except?"

"Except one for a female role's"

"What!" Surya frowned. He didn't understand why. He looked at the crowd around him. He definitely saw most of the girls of C.B.W. He thought that Varun wanted to speak with some of his own friends to act in that character. Maybe Varun was shy on speaking with girls. Surya started laughing on thinking about this.

"Varun! Look around you, there are nearly at least a hundred girls in this room! Can't you speak to at least one? Whom are you kidding now eh? Come on if you're shy I'll come and speak for you!" Surya teased Varun.

"Surya, calm down alright. I know all of the girls in C.B.W. That would be more than 10 times the numbers present here. Stop behaving like a playboy alright!" Surya stopped his laugh at once.

"If that is so, why haven't you got anyone for the role?" Surya asked.

"Man, they've got dumb rules dude, they want events to be performed by only boys or girls. None of the performances must include the participation of a girl and a boy!"

"What the hell! Who in the name of God put up these rules?" Clearly Surya was annoyed on hearing this. He hated C.B.W. for this one reason. The school did not practice co-education. Even though boys and girls were admitted, they had to be in separate class rooms. In general, the school had 4 sections in one grade. For a sixth grader, he/she would be separated in to 6th A or B or C or D. The sections A & B are for girls, and the rest, C & D were for boys.

Thus the only way to have friendship with girls was through these cultural fests. Even here, they'd put up all these restrictions. What annoyed the most was, now Surya clearly knows that he and Shivani cannot participate together. He started feeling bad, that one was his favourite choice.

"Yes, now, you know my problem. I need a boy who has to act in a girl's role." Varun said in a desperate voice to Surya. Clearly he was upset. Which boy would ever play a woman's role? Who'd wear sari in front of 31 schools, which had so many girls to make a guy scared to death.

Surya started looking around. Possibly he couldn't find Shivani. He had a friend in need before him. It was this character that God had given him which made him feel worried as well as proud. He'd lose anything for friends. He'd even start fighting his own family, to go out and stay with friends. Surya at once left all the thoughts about Shivani.

"I'll do it. Don't worry; I'll play as the female role!" Surya said with the greatest confidence he ever had.

"You sure man? If I give your name to sir, there's no backing up!" Varun said in a warning note.

"Yep, I am." Surya said with the same tone.

"You have to practise a lot"

"No problem."

"You have to really imitate a woman."

"Piece of cake, dude."

"You got to wear a sari."

"I'll ... wh... wh... WHAT!!!" Surya lost all his confidence at once.

"What? Did you think that you'll just tell the dialogues of a lady and just get out? If you got to be a lady, you must certainly look like one."

"Oh no, Sari is a really difficult thing dude."

"Okay, now I guess you're not in the skit then. I'll search for another boy, if I don't get one, I think I'll be calling off the skit and watch the other performances as an audience."

"Well, why can't you play the girl's role?"

"Seriously Surya? Are you this dumb? How in the world would anyone believe a guy like me, with this much beard and 'stash that I'm a woman huh?" Varun was really irritated on Surya's questions. He continued, "Look, are you in or are you out?"

"Alright man, I'll do it; anyway, I got no beard like you... neither a moustache."

"Good, I'll give your name."

Surya didn't see Shivani, that day, he was upset. He didn't like the change of events. He later understood that Shivani was just a messenger from some teacher who had organised an audition in the hall. She was in no way connected to the competition. She was not a competitor, nor an organiser. Well, he at least hoped for Shivani to be one among the audience, but even if she was, Shivani would see Surya in a goddamn sari!

"What was I thinking?!" Surya cursed himself for making the decision to act as a woman.

Surya really felt trapped. All he had now in the end was disappointment. He was so happy for Shivani being in an event, where he could join with her again, with all those happiness. But when he went there, he had to make a choice that someone else cherishes, where all Surya will have to do is sacrifice his happiness. God had again started his play with Surya. He gave the happiness of being with Shivani, yet finally tricked on making him do something that he didn't like. Well, Surya couldn't realise that, yet.

He was in the sadness of not seeing Shivani that evening. He didn't go to the van stand, where he could've seen her as he did every day, hoping she would be in the Gandhi hall, Surya didn't go to the van stand. While thinking of all that, Surya had been pedalling his turbo-drive slowly to Palar Club, to play badminton.

He entered the court slowly and sadly. On opening, he saw Dhanvita. As usual she was sitting at the left end corner of the badminton court's net. He didn't even care about her. She too, turned away on seeing him. Surya kept his racquet aside and kept his face supported within his palms, and looked down, blankly staring at the floor.

Seeing this, Preethi, came and asked Surya.

"What happened, Surya? You seem depressed."

"Nothing..." Surya's voice was so, low.

"Come on, tell us now!" Divya started speaking.

"Look, I can't tell you that."

"Why? Anything personal that has to be kept from us?" Preethi asked.

"No! It's not personal." Surya replied.

"*Then come on tell us.*" Divya added.

"*Alright look, I had to see one person and I couldn't find her, and that's why I'm upset. I can't tell anymore, alright...*" Surya said, and turned away from the two girls.

"*Her??*" Divya asked.

"*Who's that 'her' Surya?*" Preethi asked.

"*That 'her' is...*" Suddenly Krishna came in shouting through the doors of the badminton court, nearly breaking them by kicking it open.

"*NO! Krishna, please don't tell them! Not this time.*" Surya shouted back.

All these rupture, caught Dhanvita's attention. She started looking at the two guys, who're now making an enormous noise in the echoing shuttle hall. She was irritated, yet still curious on the topic that's going on. She didn't listen what Surya had been telling to Divya and Preethi, So, she keenly observed the on-going conversation between Surya and Krishna.

"*Why?*" Krishna asked, notoriously, acting as if he was innocent.

"*Look, Krishna, not this time. They don't have to know.*" Our startled Surya was trying to make Krishna stop, who was speaking like a fast moving train in a track.

"*Come on, Krishna tell, tell, tell!*" Preethi and Divya were encouraging Krishna to tell the name of the person referred as 'her'!

"*Please Krishna!*" Surya pleaded.

"Can I tell them Surya? Can I? Can I?" Krishna teased Surya.

We all remember that Krishna is a guy who loved spreading secrets among friends. It was Krishna who had spread it before. This situation is the best liking for a guy like Krishna. He had people begging for the secret to be revealed! And he also had the person, pleading for the secret to be maintained. Well, each and every time Krishna encounters this type of situation, He'd let out the Secret.

"Shivani!!!!!! Of 9th A!!!! Ha-ha!!!" Krishna let it. He told the name.

Two people in the court had extreme feelings on hearing this. One was Surya, he was upset. He had already encountered the bad luck of not seeing Shivani, now he had to dress up in a sari, before students from 31 schools around the district, finally, people in the club are now aware of Surya's love towards Shivani. All this had made Surya really angry on Krishna. He never liked this one thing about Krishna. Krishna was Surya's trusted friend and yet he says out the secrets shared. We can't blame Krishna too. He just shared these secrets with his friends; he found no mistake in it, which made him tell them.

Surya got out of the court angrily. He slammed the door while closing it in his anger, for which two of the screws fell in the intensity of the slam. He went out and sat in the lawn, where he had first sang the dreadful song years ago. Krishna, Divya and Preethi, first laughed a lot on hearing the news and later, after they controlled it, went out to console Surya.

Remember there were two persons who had extreme feelings on hearing Shivani's name? Surya was one and we saw his reaction, the other one was Dhanvita! Shivani was Dhanvita's best friend! Didn't we recognise that Shivani was a girl whose beauty had captured a guy like Surya, who had intentions that none of the girls in C.B.W. were pretty? We also recognised that Dhanvita was a girl who appreciated the looks of the person than their character for being friends with.

Shivani, being the prettiest one in C.B.W. was certainly the closest one to Dhanvita. Both of them were in the Hindi language club of the School, where they had become acquaintances at first. Later as days passed, Dhanvita and Shivani became good friends. Shivani had spent times in library with Dhanvita, while Shivani had prepared for quiz competitions, and Dhanvita had prepared for her regular exams in school. Whenever Shivani and Dhanvita were free, they'd go to the library, or the Hindi room. They even would come for the samosas, at the 10:50 a.m. break together. Dhanvita was so close to even Shivani's family that she could go and stay at Shivani's home for weeks without any hesitation.

Well. Coming back to our story, Dhanvita could not tolerate for, after all a guy like Surya, loving a pretty girl like Shivani. Dhanvita was so angry and irritated. She thought that Shivani deserves more than the rubbish rat Surya. She well, thought this must be handled for Shivani. She must save Shivani, from a guy like Surya! Shivani can be impressed by this beggar! Also, Shivani told that she was speech-less on seeing some boy. If a girl like Shivani likes a boy, he must be pretty handsome and so talented. He must be well built and would be an encouraging and a kind hearted person. Shivani would've chosen right! But what if Surya changes her mind? What if he cheats her? What if Surya betrays Shivani!

These thoughts passed like winds in Dhanvita's mind. She believed so much that Surya had all evil within himself which would make her best friend cry forever. So, Dhanvita started planning to make Shivani hate Surya. But for this a bigger plan must be made. Surya should not point out at Dhanvita and say 'she's the one that had planned and set me up bad before you because, she never liked me!' to Shivani. Then Shivani would mistake Dhanvita, Shivani would believe that Surya was good and Dhanvita was bad.

So, at first, Dhanvita was clear to make Surya believe that it was rather fate than her that made Shivani hate him. For that, she had to become nice with Surya. She must play a safe game, discreet on the identity and impactful in the operation. On having a clear idea of the task, Dhanvita came out of the shuttle court. She saw Surya, still upset with Krishna, sitting at the centre, and Preethi, Divya and Krishna, were around him and trying to console him. Dhanvita thought within herself.

"Don't cry Surya, Shivani will never be yours." She walked up near them.

"Why are you crying for this small thing Surya?" Dhanvita asked Surya in a kind voice.

Surya had turned to look who was saying that. Instant irritation had occupied his mind and he was even angrier for Dhanvita now knew the fact about Shivani. Yet, he was puzzled on why Dhanvita had become so kind hearted now with him.

"First of all, I'm not crying alright! Do you see any tears coming from my eyes? And second, how come you're suddenly so kind to me huh?" Surya said in a tone that could make anyone angry.

Dhanvita, though controlling her anger, continued,

"Look Surya, I know you and I are not in good terms with each other. And I'm really sick of that issue, I know I shouldn't have behaved to you that way before, that's why I've started speaking with you again. And I'm sorry for that day; I shouted back at you angrily, you were just making fun. I understood it only later. Let's be friends Surya."

Seeing Surya's reaction change from irritation to attentiveness, Dhanvita continued.

"If you don't believe me, I'll help you in making Shivani love you."

"What! You know Shivani?" Surya asked in shock.

"Yes, Shivani and Dhanvita are really close friends." Divya said to Surya.

"They even go to the Hindi club together!" Preethi added.

"Hindi club?!" Surya asked Dhanvita in confusion. He continued, "But you are Telugu right? Why do you want to learn Hindi?"

"You see, I didn't want to learn Tamil as my second language. I had no use in it. And for the lack of presence of Telugu as the second language, I chose Hindi." Dhanvita said with a sigh. She couldn't control all the dumb questions Surya asked. She never spoke this much too actually, unless she was angry.

"Oh, great, now she's going to tell this thing to Shivani, Thanks a lot." Surya whispered to Krishna.

"So, message delivered my friend." Krishna said to Surya. Clearly he didn't seem serious on Surya's issue.

"Stop it, you moron." Surya pushed Krishna away.

"Alright, look Dhanvita please don't tell Shivani anything about this topic. Never tell her, anything! I believe in telling her things myself. Don't do anything. Leave this topic." Surya told to Dhanvita.

"Are you sure Surya?" Dhanvita asked.

"Yes I am. Anyways, I'm sorry too, for that day, I shouldn't have teased you. If I had hurt you I'm Sorry."

"Oh! No it's alright Surya." Dhanvita said. Though she said these words, she thought to herself, "Uh you should be Surya! You don't know your limits. You will be sorrier soon too."

"Okay, problem solved. Let's play Shuttle. Come on guys." Krishna said. Surya frowned at Krishna's face.

"So, Surya, what happened with the auditions? Did you see Shivani? Did you speak with her?" Krishna asked Surya.

"No, I didn't see her. She was just an announcer. She had no role with the auditions." Surya replied sadly.

"What auditions?" Dhanvita asked.

"The Vaibhav auditions." Surya replied.

"Oh! It was only me and Shivani that had conducted those announcements." Dhanvita informed Surya.

"What! You were there too?"

"Yes."

"I didn't see you when Shivani was announcing? Where were you?"

"I was standing outside."

"Oh, So you guys are just messengers right? You didn't have any part in the auditions."

"No. we don't."

"Great." Surya said in a tone of disappointment.

"Ok! Enough with what we already know. Tell me what happened in the auditions Surya." Krishna interrupted the conversations.

"I went in there and found Varun. He had a skit confirmed for the competition." Surya replied with a sigh.

"So that's why grandpa hasn't come to play today. He might be perfecting his skit." Preethi said. Varun had a nick name called 'grandpa' due to his beard and stuff at this age.

"Yes. And I had to do a role in his skit. That's what I'm going to do for Vaibhav." Surya replied.

"Great! Now what's the worry in that Surya? Stage fear?" Krishna asked.

"You man, you should not even say the word Stage. You could sweat up and vomit on hearing that! Don't forget your escapade today." Surya threatened Krishna.

"Alright chill bro!" Krishna retreated.

"Come on now, tell us! Why are you still worried?" Divya asked.

"For that skit, I have to..." Surya stopped telling.

"You have to...?" everyone asked.

"Have to drape a sari and act as a woman!" Surya said it out. At once everybody in the place started laughing. Surya was embarrassed. Anyway he had already decided it's going to be a shameful incident. So he didn't take it seriously. He too gave a small laugh and had entered the Shuttle court to play. He also thought, "It will be Revolutionary!"

Chapter 10: C.C.E.

"**N**o, Surya not like that! You should say, 'Oh son, don't worry, you could come through it! You can do this. Now don't cry!' but you're saying 'Don't do this, you can come through!' Feel the difference! Now let's start from your dialogue Surya!" Varun was speaking at the highest tone of his voice. Surya, Varun and some of Varun's friends were now in Gandhi hall. They're doing a rehearsal for Varun's skit. The Skit was coined C.C.E.

The Continuous and Comprehensive Evaluation, abbreviated as C.C.E. is the new system introduced by the Central Board of Secondary Education of India in providing good quality education in schools of India. It was introduced in such a way that, Surya's batch, would experience the full System, whereas Varun's batch would just enjoy the grading system in it.

The system had impacted both positively and negatively in C.B.W. The system said that, a student must not only read the syllabus, but he must also experience it and have full knowledge about the syllabus. To facilitate the motto, the system had planned on making students do projects, take seminars, have group discussions, and do various activities a teacher set out to the children, making them easily understand topics well. Each and every task a child does is rewarded with specific grades, which add up to their F.A. called Formative

Assessment, that when added together will make up to 40% of their marks in their term end examination.

The former system of writing three term examinations, like Quarterly, Half-yearly and Annual examinations were changed to SA1 and SA2, Summative Assessments 1&2 respectively. Three terms were reduced to two and periodical assessments were conducted regularly that made scoring marks easier. Also, it had grades that evaluated a student's personal behaviour as well. There were marks for the student's well behaviour like planting trees in neighbourhood, active participation in school works, physical education trainings, etc.

Though all the systems were introduced well, a sudden change in any flow of process would certainly damage a few groups. Surya's batch, being the first to experience C.C.E., encountered problems with some students, who found it hard to adapt to it and eventually they lost some grades due to that. Also, people at C.B.W. thought they could use this system to make children follow certain rules the management wanted very easily.

With all these rules the C.C.E. had introduced, the school management made few more rules with it. Which is, Students must be in proper uniforms and polished shoes, boys must cut their hair regularly, both boys and girls must have trimmed nails, failures will have their grades in the physical education section get reduced. Boys and girls communication inside or outside the campus will have to see their personal behaviour grades reduced. Students if found speaking in any other language beside English within the school campus would have their FA in English subject reduced and if students are found riding motor bikes anywhere would have their grades reduced.

Like these, the school management bombarded the students with these extra limitations, which made a negative impact on the C.C.E. among most of the students in Surya's batch, who started hating it. Though the management considered it as shaping up the well-being of the students, the students thought that the school was poking their noses in the personal lives of the students. Well, the students couldn't fight with the management. They unwillingly followed the strict implications in the school.

Coming to the story, all these systems gave Varun the script for his skit. His skit was about a boy, who faces many problems in his school life due to C.C.E. He loses his interest in studies, he at an extent hates his life, and stops going to school, where his parents encourages on tackling the problems. Once the child had understood his parent's support, he works hard and achieves greater than before, through C.C.E.

So, it is now, understood that Surya was the mother of the boy. And Varun was training Surya with his dialogues.

"Look Surya, enough playing. Go memorize the dialogues!" Varun was now serious. He had to get this job done.

"Alright, alright… than this system, you're killing me directing it!" Surya hesitated.

After a few hours, the play was rehearsed more than ten to twelve times. Everyone was tired. So, Varun decided to finish it off and do it directly on the competition. The required efforts were done. What was incomplete now is that Varun hasn't seen Surya's costumes. Surya had to drape the sari and show it to Varun.

"Surya, Come on, let's go to your home. Tell your mom to drape the sari around you. I want to check the costumes." *Varun ordered Surya.*

"Huh! There's no way that's going to happen bro!" *Surya rejected.*

"What?"

"I don't give a damn if you want to check my costumes. I'll check for it myself. You just do the other works."

"Alright! And look! If you ever get scared on appearing on sari, and if you don't come! I'll rip you right off" *Varun said.*

"Calm down bro... I will come bye-bye!" *Surya laughed and went on to his home."*

"Maa! Help!" *Surya called out his mother to ask her teach him on how to drape a sari.*

"Yes Surya?"

"Come here! How will you tie after this?" *Surya was now tangled between two ends of the sari; he got stuck in a place where he had to fold the sari's cloth a few times above the stomach to adjust its size around the hips. He folded them in a way that in the end, they had* come to the back. It looked like Surya had grown a tail behind him, which was covered by the sari. Surya's mom came in and saw the situation. She laughed on seeing her son in such a mess.

"How many times Surya? I told you to tie it in the front!"

"Mom! I am tying it at the front, when I take the other end and put it around the shoulders, it somehow goes to the back."

"Oh, Surya do you have to do this?"

"If I don't Varun would kill me mom."

"Alright the last time, I'll tie it around you. Watch clearly and practise it properly."

Saying that Surya's mom started draping Surya the sari she had given him. She showed him the steps on the way, and later she completed her task and told Surya to keep these things in mind and go to bed. She told him that, he would do it well if he practises with a fresh mind the next day. Surya obeyed and went to his bed. He was pretty anxious for the next day. He thought about encountering the crowd in a sari. He felt a little fear.

"Oh Surya, I almost forgot. I've bought you a wig. It would suit you. Try draping the sari with that tomorrow!" Surya's mom said from the other room.

"WHAT!!!!!!!!!!!!!!!!!!!!" Surya was shocked. Sari itself was a big insult, now he also has a wig for it! All he thought was, "it's going to be a crazy day tomorrow!"

Chapter 11: Sari, in front of Shivani.

*I*t's the end of November. The perfect cold winter morning had made the birds postpone their morning chirping an hour or so. The fog that had been setting up all night has not yet lifted. The warm sun hasn't come to take them away. Even he has decided to let them play on earth for a while. The winter morning would always make people get a little more cosy within their blankets wrapped tightly around them, letting them search a small warmth wherever possible, even dogs and cats, shrugged themselves to get a little warmth, poor plants and trees, having no options of covering themselves from the cold, cried through the fog's moisture, where their tears stayed in every leaf, like small pearls in their respective oysters.

Though the atmosphere was this cold, one boy cannot feel it. He was still in the heat. He couldn't sleep well. The moisture in the air couldn't stop him. He was too occupied to even feel the chill. His head was occupied with the sense of shameful incidents that could happen in the future. So, in order to brace himself for the events to encounter, the boy woke up. The first thing he did even without brushing was seeing the wig his mom had bought. The wig's hair felt as hard as a ripped coconut's tuft. He didn't even want to hold it, but he had to keep it in his head, in front of such a crowd. So, he wanted to see himself first before the world could see. He wore it out and went to a mirror placed above the wash-basin.

"*Oi, Oi, Oi, I'm totally dead today!*" *Surya thought to himself. Well, lack of the escape option, he just let himself some guts he could find and started to get ready for the day.*

"*Mom, can you give the sari? I've to practise to drape it!*" *Surya called and went inside his parents' bedroom.*

The morning bell of the school had rung nice and clear. The participants of the Vaibhav competition were only allowed to the Gandhi hall. Others went only on permission of the teachers. The competition's inauguration had started by the first bell at 9:30 a.m. and by 10:00 o'clock they had started the competitions. The competitions were in an order. At first the singing competition was conducted, followed by dance, then short film, and the skit performance was final.

The song and dance competition itself took the first half of the day. On realising the number of performances left in the remaining two categories, the judges decided to conduct both the short films and skits simultaneously in two different venues. A classroom next to the Gandhi hall was allotted for the short film competition, and the Gandhi hall was allotted for the Skit. By 2:30 p.m., the skit performances started. Surya and his crew never saw any of the performances. The students of C.B.W. were given a separate empty classroom on the ground floor during the lunch period to practise the skit. The privilege of conducting competition in the same school facilitated this opportunity.

The performance of Surya's skit was the final most. It had to be done at approximately 3:45p.m.

Surya and every other members of the skit were ready with the costumes. Surya even now wasn't able to drape the sari. He asked a help of a teacher to do it for him. Finally, when the sari was done draped, he placed the wig and watched over the mirror. He really felt bad. His legs started Shivering. After some time he stopped worrying on his looks and was concentrating on the dialogues. All the members of the skit, though was about to laugh, controlled it to prevent startling Surya. Surya, on the other hand, seeing that no one was laughing, felt alright with the sari. He felt that he could do it. He had the confidence now.

By 3:40 p.m., a teacher had come to call the students. When he came in, the first boy he saw was Surya. He was shocked to see someone in a sari and obviously with a long hair. Nobody knew what he thought, but the frowned expression he had in his face clearly explained disgust. Surya saw him too. That look by the teacher gave Surya goose bumps. The teacher at instant broke the confidence this boy had. Seeing the disgust look in the teacher, Varun came in to change it before Surya runs away. He interrupted between the teacher's visions and asked him what the matter is about. The teacher informed them to come to the stage. And he also whispered something to Varun by the ear. Varun nodded and closed the door.

"What did he say?" Surya asked Varun. He was in real anger now.

"Nothing, we're next. They want us to come upstairs."

"That I heard. What did he whisper to you?"

"No, it's nothing Surya he didn't tell anything big."

"It's alright, tell me."

"Surya! Leave it!"

"No Varun, You now tell me the damn thing that he said to you. Did he say that I'm disgusting? Or did he tell me not to come to the competition? Or did he ask whether I was a real boy?" Surya's temper was boiling hot.

"Calm down Surya. He said to... adjust your wig, your own hair is visible at you forehead."

Everyone in the classroom couldn't control any longer. They at first found Surya in sari funny, later the wig's concept really couldn't control their laughter. They tried not to laugh at it, but when the teacher mentioned about the wig, their laugh broke through their gates. They fell to the ground while laughing. They laughed as if they won't get another opportunity to laugh. The main reason for the laugh was that, Surya was looking perfectly like a girl. That too, like a 40-50 year old. They said,

"Surya, if you were really a girl, man, some guy who'd have married you must be really lucky!" "Surya, why someone else? Marry me!" "Can we even call you Surya?" all their laughs, gave Surya irritation as well as laughter. They're tease was irritating, but even though, the

costume worked out well. That gave him happiness. He finally took it sportively. He was now not afraid of what will happen in the stage, but he was ready to face it. The crew started walking upstairs. They had the classroom in the ground floor whereas Gandhi hall was straight above it, in the first floor.

"Damn, how're they even walking with this?" Surya cursed the sari he was wearing. He could barely walk, where he now have to climb the stairs with it. He was also praying that the sari doesn't fall off to the ground in the stage which would be really embarrassing. So, with all these things playing in the mind Surya nervously entered the Gandhi hall.

The crowd inside the hall, for a moment came to a pin drop silence on seeing Surya. They never expected this! They were amazed by the perfections in the costumes taken care by the crew members. All they did was watch the people open mouthed. Surya's leg started shivering. Good thing for the sari, it didn't show his vibrating legs. Everyone after relieving from the shock, started clapping and whistled, for Surya's appearance. Even the judge clapped. They were really impressed on the courage Surya had in dressing up like that. On the other hand, the crew people were staring at the crowd. They were confused for what's happening.

"Dude, why are they clapping now itself? Do they want us to go out?" A boy asked Varun.

"What?" Varun asked in confusion.

"We usually clap only when a performance is over and when the people in it come out. But they're clapping now!"

"Will you shut your mouth and start the play?" Varun ordered.

"Alright…"

The play went on well. Surya found the people's encouragement really boosting him. He was off the fear, and was acting really well. He also had an eye on the grip of the sari. His inability to walk gave the effect of an old lady, which suited the character, which the judges believed that it was Surya's performance that's excelling even at minute parts. They thought that Surya was living the character.

Once the performance was over, everyone gave a good ovation to the performance. The judge noted that Surya did an extremely good job. And with the event concluded. They started telling the winners of the skit category. The judges announced,

"The first place goes to… Ratna Vihar CBSE School!" announced the judge.

"WHAT!" the crowd present at the hall were shocked. Everyone expected that C.B.W. would've got the first place. Everyone loved the skit and especially Surya's costume.

"Now, wait, wait, the second place goes to C.B.W. higher secondary school!" everyone cheered the people of C.B.W. they thought though second place was unfair, C.B.W. was worth the cheers. The judge continued… "Though the performance of C.B.W. was extra-ordinarily *good, they lacked co-ordination and fluent delivery of dialogues, which the people of Ratna Vihar maintained. Plus, Ratna Vihar had girls who performed the skit too."*

"What!" Surya asked Varun.

"Yes Surya, it was our school that restricted the participation of both boys and girls. Other school had their performances with boys and girls."

"Why didn't you say that to me?"

"You'd become angry. That's why."

"Well, I could have, but not anymore, look at the cheers I got! I'm now famous dude, thanks for the opportunity man."

"Well, you're welcome; our school's rules had given you that fame. I wouldn't even have approached you if the girls were allowed! Ha-ha!!" Varun laughed.

"Man I got to go out and cha..." Surya after exchanging the laugh with Varun started leaving the Gandhi hall. He was busy speaking with Varun that he hadn't noticed Shivani coming in the opposite. Shivani too, was busy with the papers in her hand and was looking through them. When they both neared, Surya nearly bumped into Shivani. He was so close to her. He couldn't believe his fate! What a pulse he got in a second! Shivani didn't realise that it was Surya, she thought that it was some ma'am that she bumped into and she

just said, 'I'm sorry ma'am' and walked away. Certainly, she was concentrating much on the papers.

Surya nearly fell to the ground in the pleasure of seeing Shivani that close. He was nearly feeling the beautiful aroma of his Shivani. Her golden glittered ear-rings were just a centimetre away from his eyes. Her hair was caressing his face from left to right. She influenced the whole soul of Surya. Surya was magnetised in the strong field that Shivani had produced on him. Surya was breath-less, speech-less and was just seeing Shivani pass through the corridor.

"Wow! The happiest day in my life!!!!!!!!!!!!!!!!!!!!!!!!!" Surya started screaming! He jumped in excitement! He stretched his arms and closed his eyes to feel the effect that Shivani produced again. In time, while he was landing, Surya felt something like a cloth making him slip and fall to the ground. Only after the fall, Surya realised,

"I'm in the Goddamn sari!!!!!!!!!!!!!!!!!!!!! Ohhh Goddddd!!! Why? Why me? Why this has to happen? Why is the best moment of my life happening in the worst costume that I would ever wear? Ohhh!!!!!!!!!!!!!" Surya cursed himself.

"I'm sorry ma'am" Varun teased Surya. Surya stared at him angrily. Varun continued…"Dude, I thought you were getting praises for wearing this, don't you remember? You even thanked me! Now why are you angry?"

"Oh shut up, now come on, let's go and change this shit." Surya said.

"Alright!" Varun laughed and accompanied Surya.

Chapter 12: First talk

The evening sun that was about to go to rest, after a day's hard work, sharing it's light to the people it saw, tired of the travel to the west, started to depart to his home to let some room for his friend 'the moon' do the adornment of the sky after he went. The sun's friends in earth, wanted to make the day's farewell to him in an unforgettable and beautiful manner. They wanted him to have a colourful farewell as they did on each and every sunset. They thought and thought and finally, came up with a mild, soothing orange colour. The sun, too, considering the efforts of his friends to disperse his light, wanted not to harm them with much brightness and went on for milder amplitude on his sharing.

Through the pleasant lights provided by these friends by the window, two of our friends, who just had success hugging them and making them proud, went to the classroom that was in the ground floor. They started to change their dresses. Our friend Surya decided to stay in the t-shirt. He didn't want to change to the uniform. Anyway, school was already over. He didn't have anyone to question him about the T-shirt. So, when he packed everything in the bag, and was about to leave, a new friend, called Vignesh came out calling Surya. Vignesh was Surya's classmate. He was coming as if Surya was long sought and finally found. Surya noticed Vignesh and went up to him.

"What's up dude?" Surya questioned.

"Dude, I came from our class through the Hindi room and…"

"…And?"

"Dude, Shivani was alone in the Hindi room! This is a great time for you to speak with her! Come on let's go!"

"What? Man, you're not playing with me are you?"

"No man, I definitely saw her! Are you coming with me or not?"

"Alright, I'm in. Varun, please wait right here. I'll be right back!" Surya said to Varun.

"Yea, it's alright man, all the best!"

"Thanks, bye!"

"Come on dude, we don't have any time to waste." Surya said to Vignesh. Surya was barely walking. He was running.

C.B.W. school building was an electronic eight-shaped. There were two long parallel corridors, which were intersected by three perpendicular small corridors, two at the ends and one in the middle. The room, in which Vignesh saw Shivani, was in the top-left corner of the school when looked at a bird's-eye-view. Our boy Surya was now at the bottom-right. Surya rushed in through the staircase hall, ran through the corridors, jumped through the bushes in the garden between the ways and finally reached to the door of the Hindi room, where Shivani was sitting alone.

The boy, who came in rushing from the far end of the school, in a matter of two minutes, now found it difficult to cross the doors of the Hindi room. Vignesh who was beside Surya was persuading Surya to go in and speak with Shivani.

"Come on Surya, All the best dude! Rock it man!" Vignesh said to Surya.

"Yea? You think I can make it?" Surya asked.

"Yes! Why not?"

"Yeah! Why not? I'm going in…" Surya on saying this to Vignesh went near the door of the Hindi room. He peeped at Shivani. She was sitting by the end, near the window. Surya was paralysed. He couldn't even think of going in. He didn't even think of anything, he just stood there and enjoyed Shivani's beauty. Suddenly he heard someone tap him by the shoulder. He suddenly turned in shock.

"Surya! Go and speak man!" Vignesh said.

"Oh, man! You gave me a heart attack! Yes I will go… wait and watch." Surya said. He let in a long breathe and started walking furiously towards the door. Vignesh watched him go and while he was watching, Surya, with the same speed, came back to Vignesh. Away from the Hindi room!

"What the hell did you do now?" Vignesh asked in shock.

"If I go there, what should I speak?"

"*Speak anything. Introduce yourself, ask about her, and tell her your feelings, anything! Go speak man, this is a once in a life time opportunity.*"

"*Okay got it!*" saying that, Surya went back. Vignesh was in the opposite end of the corridor, watching Surya go. Surya passes the library and was at the door of the Hindi room. Again, Surya came back.

"*OH YOU MORON!*" Vignesh scolded Surya! He became impatient with the games Surya's playing. "*Why can't you just go in and speak?*"

"*Man, wow, I cannot speak man, She's so beautiful, her eyes, her face, ahhh, it paralyses me dude, how could I speak?*" Surya said with a sigh.

"*This is bullshit! Now if you don't go in and start speaking with her, sure there'll be another guy who'd make her love him instead. Who knows if she's already in love?*"

"*Shut up! There can't be anything like that! Shivani's meant to be with me! You don't know how it feels, it's magical! That feeling you won't even realise with anyone else, except for the one who is meant to be with you!*"

"*So, if it's magical, why can't you go do abracadabra with her? Now, shut up and go speak.*"

"*Alright, this time I'd speak for sure.*" Surya went back again, for the third time. This time, on seeing the speed, Vignesh thought that Surya would surely go in. Surya crossed the library swiftly. There were two *pillars in between the doors of the library and the Hindi room. Surya crossed the first pillar... the second one... and finally it's the door of the Hindi room! Surya also... went PAST the Hindi room with the same speed. He went to the opposite side and saw Vignesh. Clearly, Surya was afraid. Surya couldn't speak. Vignesh, on seeing Surya's face started laughing. Surya looked like a pug, that's waiting for its food, big eyes, about to cry. Vignesh came to Surya. While crossing the Hindi room, he glanced at Shivani. Surya saw Vignesh laughing at him. Surya was worried about his inability.*

"Look Surya, now don't worry. Just go in and ask her if she has seen you before. Ask her if she knows you, and then, tell her the 'Heal the World' performance and tell her your feelings. If any teacher comes by, I'll let you know."

"You sure?"

"Yes, now I'll watch and you go in. Carry whatever guts you have in yourself. And go speak with her Surya! It's now or never!"

"Okay!" Surya said. He again breathed in and went. This time Surya went inside the Hindi room successfully. He saw Shivani writing something. He saw the Hindi room board squeezed with nearly the whole year's portion the student's going to study. He then saw her back. Shivani too, at this time, saw Surya enter the room. Both of them made a straight eye to eye contact! What scenery it was... her eyes, the ones that had always killed Surya, which burnt his soul at every instant, which made him paralysed... those which that even *the lord Brahma found amazed on his own creation. Surya felt that as if he had got the direct blessing from God himself. He noticed the sunlight that peeped between her hairs... and whatever that came through, got stuck in the ear-ring clashed within it again and again and finally came out in all directions. Even light seems to get startled and get shattered in her presence. She illuminated all of light that touched her. These entire feelings, made Surya smile wanly at Shivani. Shivani couldn't understand why Surya has come. So she asked, "Yes?"*

Surya got back to Earth. But though, he couldn't control himself. His voice was trembling. He tried to control and spoke,

"Do you know...?"

"Pardon?" Shivani interrupted. She couldn't hear what Surya was telling. She was Surprised on what a stranger could ask to her. She didn't expect him to come either. She couldn't make out any guesses to what Surya said. He was barely opening his mouth. But Surya thought that Shivani had deduced what he was going to tell, and she wanted him not to say anything else because of which she had interrupted him speaking. So, Surya, immediately, stupidly, changed the topic.

"Do you know... where our library sir is?" Surya, shouted out loud, with his voice trembling.

"Library sir? You mean... librarian?" Shivani asked.

"Y... Yea"

"I don't know. I haven't seen him yet." Shivani replied with a shrug.

"Okay, thanks bye!" Surya, saying this, didn't even stop for Shivani's reply; he jolted through the doors, and out went walking fast, nearly running, to the chemistry lab, nearly 50-feet away. Vignesh saw Surya come through the doors, and whizzing off from him. He ran to Surya and asked,

"Whoa, man! Congrats! What happened? How was your first conversation?" He asked with a lot of excitement.

"I went to her. . ." Surya panted.

". . .and?"

". . .asked her. . ." He panted again for breath, to escape from shock.

". . .and?" Vignesh ogled his eyes, opened it full, waiting for Surya to tell what happened. He held Surya's shoulders, encouraging him to tell.

"She told that she hasn't seen the librarian yet!"

"WHAT!?" Vignesh frowned. Vignesh dropped his arms from Surya's shoulders.

"I didn't ask her if she knew me. . . I asked her where our librarian was!"

"Are you out of your mind? Why did you come up with such a damn thing?"

"Man, you won't understand. That moment. . . that moment when you look into her eyes. . . you just completely forget everything else man. . . that too, with the excitement it provides, when those eyes look

at you straight... God... I'll go speechless... plus, when she spoke to me! No one would ever know how it felt... I couldn't say it! It was like... something that makes you explode! It pumped my adrenaline dude! I couldn't control myself! I don't even know if I had really said anything in there! I feel like there were clouds all over us! I couldn't see anything! The sun... man, it illuminated her! She was like a diamond, dude... sparkling! Man, I could speak on her forever!"

Vignesh let out a long breath. He shook his head in disappointment. He didn't like the way it ended. He just took his school bag, and walked away from Surya, bidding a good-bye. Surya just stood there watching Vignesh leave.

"Surya...?" Vignesh called. When Surya looked at him, he replied, "...you really are good Surya. If she had heard all this from you, you could've got bright things happening around you. Get the guts Surya. Try to control yourself and start speaking with her. Don't be late Surya..."

Vignesh's words were so true. He's the only person that had ever given Surya the right advice for the time. Well, his word was so true, that it was the only way for Surya to get to Shivani. It was fate's clue for what Surya had to do. But, fate's actions were far more influencing than its clues.

Chapter 13: Quattuor Domos

*I*t was a sunny afternoon. The bus was travelling in a road that was in between two rows of pine trees lined up parallel to the road. The sun's rays, coming through the leaves of the pine trees, fell in the right side of the bus and eventually on its passengers seated by the window. It appeared that there was an image that had formed from light refracted through waters. Blotches of light rays would fall into motion with lines of shadows, when light falls in water and reflected. Whereas in the bus, big blotches of shadows covered the side with few lines of light rays that has passed in without any interruption.

The whole area was lit up in a pure white colour. The places outside the bus were flushing green, with traces of brown. The areas inside the bus were mostly brown from the rusted iron, and had grey leather seats for the lucky passengers who would get a chance to sit. Two young people got the chance and sat. The one near the window was admiring the playful, innocent painting that nature has created. The one next to her adored the painting that admired the other stuffs as paintings.

"Nature's wonderful right?" Shivani asked.

"Yes… really. It had created wonders. A lot… the greatest wonder it had given, is letting mankind realise the beauty it had offered." Surya replied.

"Yes! That's the main thing. I don't know if you can look outside. The window's small and I'm blocking your view Surya." Shivani said.

"No! I really have the clear view of the beauty nature has created!"

"How? Even I can't see it to the full." Shivani, saying this, stretched out to see clearly. Surya held her hand gently and spoke...

"I'm not speaking about the beauty outside. There's nothing out there..."

"Nothing?" Shivani frowned. She, for a moment thought that Surya didn't have taste for such things. Surya continued to finish his statement.

"... Compared... to the most beautiful one sitting next to me inside this half-rusted bus." Surya smiled looking at Shivani. She blushed on hearing his words.

"Oh, don't lie, Surya."

"No, I'm telling the truth. I swear!"

"Would you cut that out?" Shivani blushed. She turned away, smiling at the window. Later she turned back to Surya and continued...

"You're speaking this much Surya... why haven't you told me anything before?"

"No man can have the guts to tell this without her acceptance Shivani... I literally was scared to death. But I knew I won't die without saying all these to you!"

"Come on, easy… why speaking about all that… Am I really that special Surya?"

"Yes Shivani, yes!"

"What yes? Yes? Get out or I'll kick you off the bed!" Shouted Hari.

"Huh!! What??" Surya got up from the dream and was confused with what's happening. It took him few minutes to come to senses and realise that what he felt was a dream. But, he must need years, to come off the feeling the dream had given. What a dream was it for Surya! He waited for nearly two years for this to come true. He's still waiting though and also, it's now a really long time.

It's now the November of 2010. Surya is now in tenth grade… the first step for college in the Indian schooling system. He has to go through with the public exams this year to show his rank among the whole country practising the syllabus offered by the Central Board of Secondary Education. It's been a lot of days since Surya had put on the sari. Surya has changed a lot from that place. His world started to gain the speed, and has also given him bonuses that he ought to have at this time, for all his works. Let's have a look at our boy shall we?

Surya has grown thinner. Not because of anything else, but his very own badminton. He's become a notified boy in C.B.W. though the teachers started to become fond of Surya, the guys who mocked him when he was fat still does it. His closest friend was still Krishna, yet the counts increased with the adding up of Divya, Preethi, Akansha, Neha and Dhanvita. All the days now, these Children walk to home with Surya and Krishna each and every day. They'd slowly walk from the school, reach to the junction, which separates the streets to everyone's respective home and speak for nearly an hour or so and then leave to home. Surya has become a regular player at the Palar Club and has expertise in Badminton as well as in friendship among the people. Surya, did start to become cute as he was before in his childhood, but now had to put on the specs due to his recent myopic eye. Well, yet Surya's relationship with Shivani, never changed. He still didn't speak with her.

"Why did you wake up Hari!?" Surya asked in immense anger.

"Look at the time! Mom's already scolding; get up and brush! You have to go to school this Saturday! Lucky for me! I get to sleep all day! Every Saturday and Sunday a holiday chap! Its college little bro!"

"Yea… yea… Shut up!" Surya wrapped around his blanket and threw it in Hari's face and went out of the room.

It's the social science period for 10th D. Students are now in a pin-drop silence listening to Mr Philips' voice. His loud and pitchy voice made everyone afraid of him. Only few people could even stand up to him and speak loudly. He was a strict teacher. He never liked dis-obedient activities children does and would make them cry -not by beating but- just by looking. Surya, as usual, was next to Pravin and was in the last but one bench, sat straight and looked at the teacher blankly as *he walked to and fro in the classroom and Surya was so very sleepy, when the teacher turns his back, Surya would close his eyes 90% to give them a rest and would open them when Mr Philip turns back.*

"Dude!" Krishna whispered to Surya, pulling his shirt to call him.

"What bro...?" Surya replied in a husky voice... He was clearly sleeping.

"Now you better wake up or I'll call Sir!"

"Okay man, I'm up! Tell me."

"Look man, the inter-house badminton match is up. You want to be in?"

"Yea! Sure dude! Why not?"

"Then get up and ask Sir's Permission to leave for practise. Ask for me too!"

"What! No way! Get out!"

"Look, Surya this is our once in a life time opportunity man, we'd not go next year. First of all, we won't even be in this school next year!"

"Yea all right, but I won't ask man."

"Oh you! I know how to make you speak...! SIR!" Krishna called out Philip Sir. He turned to see who called, and Krishna continued, "Sir, Surya wants to tell something."

"Why can't Surya open his mouth and ask for himself? Are you his messenger eh?" Mr Philip scolded Krishna and turned to Surya.

"Sir, it's... it's..."

"Don't waste my time. Say it!"

"Sir, I and Krishna have to go to the practise session for the inter-house badminton match sir."

"Are you asking me or telling me?"

"Sir... I'm asking sir, obviously, ask... asking for your permission."

"Okay. You may go." Surya alone went at first. Later Krishna followed.

"Mr Messenger!" Mr Philip called out for Krishna. Krishna turned.

"I asked only him to go. Not you."

"But sir, he and I are playing together!"

"He'll get a nice partner. You come and sit!"

Surya went out and laughed at Krishna. Krishna put his head down and started marching slowly to his seat.

"Students..." Mr Philip continued his lectures. Krishna sat irritated. Sir smiled at Krishna sometimes in between his talks and continued for five more minutes. Later, he said,

"You may go Mr Messenger."

"Phew... Thank you very much Sir."

"Now go fast or I'll call you in again."

"Yes sir, Right away." Krishna, took his bag, and went running to catch up with Surya. Krishna was now the victim for Philip sir's plays. He was cursing him on the way, while he was running.

Krishna later caught up with Surya. He and Surya went to the same old Palar club, where the friends play every day. The boys went to their homes, took their racquets, and came to the court where the selection had taken place. Everyone knew that selections are a part of competition in C.B.W. it will be mostly clear from the performances in these selections, for the winner at tournament.

With all these thoughts tuned up, and ready to be fired, the friends, entered the hall. The hall was filled with students. From the trouser wearing toddlers, to the full pant fellows of each and every houses of the school were crowded respectively in their places with whatever the bat they could afford to. I think this is the perfect time to introduce the housing system of C.B.W. The school's houses were four. The houses were named after the four dominant elements of the earth- Earth, fire, wind and water. These were named in Latin, by the English teachers, to give the names an antique style, which are:

1. Water –Aqua. 2. Fire – Ignis.

3. Wind – Aura. & 4. Earth – terra

These four houses' names were really catchy for the students to hold onto it. Surya and Krishna both belonged to the house of fire element, Ignis! Their house colour was Yellow, depicting the natural flame's colour. They wore their house t-shirts and entered the hall and searched for the boys in yellow. They found the boys at the far left end of the badminton court. They straight up went to the house captain, Rakesh. When these boys approached him, he straight away recognised Krishna and spoke...

"Who's the other one?"

"He is..." *Krishna said, pointing towards Surya.*

"Do you play? Really??" *Rakesh asked.*

"Yes I will."

"Good, now let's select the students formally." *Rakesh went over the stage and started announcing the start of the selections, to all the students and went on to speak with his other fellow house captains.*

"What does he mean by saying formally?" *Surya asked Krishna.*

"Dude, we are already selected for the tournament. He just has to show people that we were selected."

"What! How are we selected without even performing?"

"Man, that guy, Rakesh... he and I are real friends dude, he has seen me play... plus there are no real players in the Ignis house. It's just you, me and Rakesh. So, all he has to do is reject whoever's coming.

Anyway, the decisions are not announced here, but in the notice board. Who the hell would know our name in this crowd eh? So let's just sit and watch."

"Great, dude! Really... awesome" Surya exclaimed. He was happy. He just has to watch others play, to see him get selected!

"Can we go then? We don't need to stay anyway..." Surya asked Krishna.

"No Surya, watch the game. You have to check others for the final tournament's competition. You need to see their game, for you to experience their play. The decision's been made only to our Ignis house; still the other damn houses are there."

"Alright!"

Surya and Krishna sat by the corner of the Shuttle court. They were unnoticed, but they noticed everything. In the Terra house, Varun was selected and another boy of Surya's class was selected. His name was Karthik. Karthik was Surya's deadliest rival. Well, they were friends from the outside. But Surya always had a cold war within him with Karthik. As we all know, Surya was born cute, but he didn't grow into a handsome whereas Karthik was a playboy in the tenth grade. No girl would ever want to talk to Surya on her own, but every girl would at least want a talk with Karthik. The main reason was, Karthik was lean, had a bass voice, and absolutely charming. Surya always wanted to be like Karthik, in which of the inability, Surya hated Karthik. This feeling developed the anger and rivalry feeling in Surya for

Karthik. Surya is now thinner, when compared to the obese body he had till his ninth grade but the thinness that girls were attracted from Karthik, was an impossible task for Surya to achieve.

Surya also found a style in Karthik's body language. His whole activities can be compared to the greased motions of pistons and gears in machinery. The simple wave he found did not come into Surya's flesh. The main image the lean bodies gave was, it would show an image of a strong hand, being ripped with the nerves all over, providing a rigid view by the bones, and the perfect, robotic shaped body, which would level a ruler to draw a straight line, again showed the same rigid support that also gave the strong image. These lean bodies would allow people to use any styles of dressing that would create more peculiar attraction at times. Well, to sum up, Surya envied Karthik for all that he had, and for all that Surya was denied of.

Well, coming back to story, Surya saw Karthik being selected. Surya's eyes focused on Karthik. Surya thought that this would be the best time to take out Karthik and show the school who's best. Surya would have his revenge by making Karthik lose in the battle. This would be the ultimate pleasure of all time. Surya started flying off with his thoughts in his imagination. He imagined on Karthik losing to Surya and threw his bat away in anger and started crying in the court for his loss and later, Surya could go and say 'better luck next time' with a grin indicating his threaten. Where Surya would eventually make Shivani realise the talent Surya had in sports and would make her come and talk to him and start a beautiful journey of love together and travel to places where love's been celebrated. Surya, day dreaming all this, stared at the court's ceiling, blankly... as if his thoughts were in motion there, where Surya's life was going through with his love Shivani and their happy ride to the land of love.

Chapter 14: The badminton game.

"*Hey Surya, Heard you're doing extremely well with sports nowadays...*" *Divya said to Surya.*

"*Well, I'd like to think so...*" *Surya felt flattered. Surya, Divya, Preethi, Akansha, Neha, Krishna and Dhanvita were walking from school to home. In the same evening that Krishna and Surya had walked over an year ago, where Krishna introduced Surya to badminton and eventually all the friends who were now precious jewels to Surya. All of them were more than friends to each other, they had the precious bond that can never be explained through friendship or brotherhood or anything. They had the laughs and lights that friendship could give, they had the love a brother would have on his younger sister and the same way of a sister's in her brother, they had the trust that a family gives, the security a dad would give, the comfort a mom gives. They had the best people among each other, who'd always have their backs on each other, clearly defining the word friendship. Yet, still, Dhanvita had the same anger on Surya, which can be stated as a talent of Dhanvita to hide the anger or Surya's trust in her that he couldn't find them.*

"*I've seen you play Surya, before and even now...*" *Dhanvita spoke. "I could see a rapid increase in your performance recently. How're you doing that? Any fire from within to succeed?*"

"Yea! Fire! I knew I smelled something burning. It was you Surya!"
Neha said.

"Oh come on..." Surya blushed.

"Or, it would've been challenging Karthik. You know how Surya hates
him!" Akansha started to speak.

"Will you stop it?" Surya ordered, pleaded to be precise.

"Oh stop it guys, It would be Shivani!" Preethi interrupted. Dhanvita's
smile which she maintained till now, smoothly evaded. "Surya would plan
on speaking with her after he wins. Like a king from war with victory!"
Preethi teased. The king dialogue was often said by Surya for his first
appearance he wants to plan on speaking normally with Shivani.

"Okay, I'll say the secret of this improvement alright? Will you all
stop this guesses?" Surya said everyone was expecting this situation.
They knew Surya would tell. Seeing their instant attention, Surya
continued... "I always imagine that Shivani sits on the court and
watch me play. That way, I could show off myself and I could impress
her. That was the way I improved! End of story."

"That's it?" Preethi asked

"Yes"

"No fire?" Dhanvita asked.

"No."

"No Karthik?" Akansha asked.

"Nope."

"How do you do this Surya?" Dhanvita asked.

"Look, my love for Shivani can't be measured. It's way above the size of the universe. No one can separate me and Shivani. We may not speak now, but I'm sure Shivani will be my love. I can assure you, even if Gods fail to protect her, I will be there. Even if it costs my life, I would happily give away, for Shivani to be happy."

"Nice memory. Saw those dialogues in yesterday's movie. Good recital Surya!" Neha teased Surya with a yawn, indicating her boredom of Surya's flimsy dialogues.

"You say that no one can separate you two?" Dhanvita intervened.

"Yes. No one can. I and Shivani are meant to be together! And it will be so."

"What non-sense? I myself can separate you two."

"No you can't!" Surya said to Dhanvita. He thought Dhanvita was playing with Surya. She too just reacted for his flimsy dialogues were his thoughts. Poor boy, didn't know that Dhanvita was already in motion of that task.

"Yes I can. I bet I can separate you two." Dhanvita said.

"I bet you can't!" Surya teased.

"Okay! 10 bucks bet!" Dhanvita continued.

"Alright!"

"Deal."

"Okay, meet you in the court Surya!" Preethi said, leaving to her home. Neha, Divya, Akansha and Dhanvita left too. Surya and Krishna started walking to the diversion that leads each other to their homes.

"You shouldn't have bet Surya… with Dhanvita." Krishna said, in a worried voice.

"Oh, that's nothing man, she just played. I too said for fun."

"From, her looks, I feel that it's not a game Surya."

"Come on man, I and Dhanvita are real friends now. She won't do that."

"What if she does for the bet?"

"What for ten bucks she'd separate me from Shivani? She knows I'll be broke bro. She won't do those things to me!"

"Dude! I've known her more than you! She's never this type! I'm noticing her being a fake friend to you. A girl like Dhanvita would never be this close with guys like us! Say even Karthik has little chance but not US!"

"Come on man, she's close to us because her friends are our best friends!"

"Close with you not to me!" Krishna said flat.

"Wait, now are you saying that she is in love?"

"Stop it you idiot! This is your problem! You're over-whelming things before you even know them! What I meant to say was... she is showing a fake closeness to somehow separate you from Shivani."

"Dude, come on! She's the one who at first told me that she'll unite me with Shivani. Why would she try to separate me?"

"Well, I don't know that Surya! But I'll just say this... This is the Universal friendship-love-help secret... Each and every boy would always try to help a friend in love. Each and every girl would always try to break the love in the friend. Understand this!" Krishna panted, exhausted of explaining Surya.

"Whatever man, all I believe is that, Shivani will be with me no matter what! I trust in that!"

"Let at least God make you realise. I got to go now... bye, see you at PC."

"Bye."

Surya on his way to home thought about the things that Krishna had said to him. He believed his talks. There was truth in them. But he trusted Dhanvita too. Surya didn't know which side he has to pick. He just left the topic and went home to refresh himself and go back to PC. This was the last day that Surya could practise for the badminton match the next day. He must practise hard this day.

The lights were lit. The wood has been swept off from dust. The floor illuminated the colour of plywood indicating that it was ready for the match. The net's strength and height was checked by the physical education teacher. The amount of shuttlecocks was checked by his assistant to govern their use in the match. Each team's players were seated already. The first match was scheduled to be played by Terra and Aqua houses. Later the houses of Ignis and Aura had to play. Teams in red were Aura, green were Terra, blue was Aqua and we already knew that Yellow was Ignis. Participants of each houses were to put on their house t-shirts while they play. Everyone was already in their costumes.

Surya and Krishna watched over Varun and Karthik in green and sitting in the opposite. For Surya it was one of his best friend and his fiercest rival in the opposite. Yet, Surya didn't pay attention to these small feelings and was concentrating in reducing his nervousness to play a good game. He was closing his eyes and was praying. He in a few minutes opened his eyes and felt relieved. He had a confidence come in from somewhere that silently told him that he was the winner that day. Surya loved the feeling. It made him taste victory. He felt happy. He had got over the fears and was now relieved.

When the Physical education teacher called the Terra and Aqua houses to start the match, Surya watched Karthik carefully. He registered each and every moves of Karthik in the game. He found his weaknesses *and his powers. Karthik indeed was a difficult guy to win, but he's not impossible to win.*

"Dude, I want you to concentrate fully on our Varun. Karthik's mine!" Surya said to Krishna, who was also watching the match.

"Next match we'll be playing with Aura Surya. It's Sundar and Mahesh in that team."

"Oh don't be dumb Krishna; we can take over those guys. I'm speaking about the final."

"Don't have over-confidence. Though you may win, it would make you lose."

"Alright…"

The match played by Terra and Aqua was ended with the scores 21-16. With Terra house, that is, Varun and Karthik's team winning. The teacher called the Ignis and Aura houses to the match. Surya and Krishna stood to their positions. Surya and Krishna followed the side-by-side partnership. They took care of their respective left and right sides of their court. They always baited for a smash from the opponent and would end the game by placing a point rather than hitting it and becoming tired. With the very same technique, they finished the match quickly. They ended up with a score of 21-13. They won with an extreme difference. They played in a great team-work. Surya already felt winning the finals, and beating off Karthik.

There was a ten minute break, for the final match. Surya and Krishna went out the court for a drink of water. They spoke how easily they won, and how easily they could bring an easy victory later. Surya taught Krishna the weaknesses he encountered on Karthik and asked on for Krishna's suggestion in taking him down. Surya and Krishna discussed strategies with the progress of the match. They had planned on front-back combo in this match. When they were coming, after being discussed their strategies, came in and noticed Mr George, master of the Ignis house speaking with the physical education teacher. The house captain, Rakesh was there too. There was also a ninth grader who was listening to the teachers. Krishna called Rakesh.

"What happened bro?" Krishna asked.

"I'm sorry to say this, but the team is now changed."

"What! Now?? Rakesh we've just won against Aura house! They can't change the team now? They don't have the time to keep a re-match with the new players!" Surya asked, puzzled.

"Look I'm sorry Surya. But I have to tell you two important things. One… they are not planning for a re-match against the auras. They will just continue with the finals. Two… they are not re-placing players."

"What do you even mean?" Krishna asked.

"They are re-placing only one player, and that would be you Surya." Rakesh said.

"*What!!*" *both the friends exclaimed in shock.*

"*Yes. Surya will be taken out and Mr George's son Andy would play in place of Surya.*"

"*Why are they doing this to me?*" *Surya asked desperately.*

"*Look Surya, Krishna's been playing for years for our house. He could win even without you. But you can't win without him. That's why they've changed you and...*" *Rakesh went on reasoning with Surya but Surya no longer heard his words. His mind went into a thought. It silenced all his senses that interacted with the physical world. He couldn't bear the injustice he's been pushed into. His talent was not respected. He just was fooled by a simple politics of a father who misused his power as a house master.*

Surya started walking. He put his head down and took his racquet and silently started walking to school... which is just a few blocks away from the Palar Club. He had his bag in his shoulders and his racquet across him and just walked through the cold winter breeze that caressed him. It was not only his soul, but the whole world is now cold by the sadness of this poor child. He walked and walked with just his head the same way it was at first, facing deep to the ground. His dream was shattered into pieces. His talent was played around and broke by people who don't even know its price. Surya slowly, went to his class, 10th D and sat on his desk, without a sound. His friends in class came and asked about the match and why Surya was silent.

Surya never replied. He just put his face on the bench and faced the trees beyond the windows.

That day, Surya never ate. He didn't speak to anyone. He just sat silent. Later in the evening after the final bell, he went out of the campus, started walking to home. He would usually wait for Krishna, Preethi, Divya, Akansha, Neha and Dhanvita to go with them. But this day, he didn't wait. He walked on. Later, he heard people calling him. Surya was two streets away from school. He turned and looked. Krishna, Neha, Akansha, Preethi and Divya were standing near a tree. Surya went near them.

"Can we leave?" He asked in a low voice.

"Yes we can." Preethi said and everyone walked slowly.

"You were supposed to wait." Neha said.

"Sorry, I forgot." Surya said.

"Come on Surya, I heard what happened in the game. Krishna said everything. Don't worry Surya. Everything will be alright." Divya said, to cheer Surya up.

"Hmmm…" Surya just hummed.

"Snap out of it Surya, come on, let's go and eat Pani Puri!" Akansha said, trying to call Surya to distract him from the sadness. But Surya rejected the call and started walking. Everyone walked silently behind him. Krishna was expecting Surya to ask a question and waited for it. And as he expected, Surya asked it a moment later.

"Who won the match?" He asked.

"Terra house." Krishna said.

"Were they too powerful?"

"No, I had the chances in my hand. The game was an easy win. Karthik was tired. He couldn't help Varun much." Surya turned on hearing this from Krishna.

"Then how did they win?" Surya asked, for the first time, his voice little high.

"I decided to lose the match." Krishna said.

"Why?" Surya asked. His voice trembled with shock and anger of losing the easy opportunity.

"I could've won this match Surya, But if I had won, your effort in recognising Karthik's weakness and your effort in winning the first match would've gone for that damn George's kid. I don't need certificate of winning without my friend! That's why I decided to lose the game."

"Yes Surya, Krishna has been telling us how quiet you became and how bad you felt. We too, support Krishna. Friends are more important Surya." Preethi said.

Surya broke into tears. He controlled anger for so long, to go and punch his pillow and cry loud over the bed, to release the anger that he had developed on the court. He feared that if he cries in school, it would make him look weak. People would tease for Surya crying like a girl. I never know who said a cry was for girls... even boys would have hurt feelings. Their hearts too, would be healed by cry, they too have to cry to let out the sadness, but our society has brought up by so many brave men who made emotions a girl's property. Anyway, Surya couldn't control his tears. He was broke. His tears came out as waters that came through a burst dam. He went and hugged Krishna, his best friend, A friend who's rare to find, rarer to understand and also extremely caring and kind.

"Thanks Krishna. Thank you all for being here with me!" Surya said to everyone.

"Yea, yea, I hate publicity dude. Now get off me before someone thinks badly!" Krishna said, tapping his Shoulder.

"Remember Surya, We'll always be there for you as your back-up don't worry! All you have to do is buy us pani-puris." Divya said.

"Yea, but it was Akansha's deal, anyway, today I will sponsor! You are my best friends, guys, I love you all. By the way, where's Dhanvita?"

"She's in library, for some works, she told she'd catch up in PC" Akansha said.

Chapter 15: The plot thickens…

*W*hile Surya embraced Krishna with the most love he had in his friends, with the happiest feeling of being loved, with the weightlessness he had in his heart, with the clarity he found in his mind, with the decision of doing anything for Krishna, Preethi, Divya, Akansha and Neha… There had been a plot that had started against all the happiness these feelings provided, a plot that is fuelled by a simple misunderstanding, by someone called Dhanvita. For every action there's an equal and opposite reaction, is what Newton has said. It's not only newton's law of forces, but it's the most basic law of nature as well.

Surya's happiness has got to an extremity, which needs to be balanced now. Dhanvita and Shivani were in the Library. Both were studying in their respective interests. Surya's badminton incident happened a few days ago. Later on, he never missed any of his time with his friends in Palar Club. He started feeling that Dhanvita was real friendly now and shared all the feelings he had about Shivani. She too, got that information clearly and stored them in her memory. It's time to start executing the plan she had made. First, she must tell Shivani that a boy loves her. Hearing that, she will -like any other girl- would get curious on whom that is. Then she would tell the characteristics of the boy and his character, which is sure to be bad. Later, she would tell that it was Surya on placing a clean bad image about him and *finally, all Dhanvita had to do was fuel the irritation with some more bad images of Surya and to part her from him forever.*

"What would you do if someone loves you Shivani?" Dhanvita asked. She had started the execution.

"Love me?"

"Yea"

"Well, I'd reject for sure! Come on! I'm just in 10th grade and plus, we've got studies! We can't roam around jobless! We've got things to do!"

"Without even knowing who that is?" Dhanvita quizzed, wanting to the exact stand of Shivani.

"I don't care, whoever that may be!"

"...But what about the guy who made you speech-less?"

"Stop it Dhanvita! I'm not saying I'm having a feeling for him! It's just once and I may have had something struck in my throat! I went on saying for three classes continuously! Just because I got stuck that doesn't mean I'm having a crush on him!"

"Ok! Ok! Cool!" Dhanvita consoled Shivani, who was actually boiling red and later continued,

"Well, you know the guy I told you that I hate the most in the world?"

"Yea, you haven't shown him to me either."

"Well, not necessary we became friends or to be precise, acquaintances."

"Good start! It's nice that you do not hate someone."

"Well, after speaking with him for few times, he just said that he's in love with you!"

"WHAT!" Shivani was shocked.

"Yeah. Even I was shocked."

"Who's that?"

"I don't think I'm going to say that, you're already tempered. You read I'll tell you later."

"How do you think I'm going to read after you said something like this?"

"That's your problem! You said you'd reject anyone? Then why do you worry?"

"Look that was my reply to your question of the aftermath of a proposal! I would've known the guy, would've stayed away from him! Now, I am curious! To know who that is! Can you understand?"

"Sort of, Okay, I'll give you a clue. He was a guy, who had already spoke with you! That's it!"

"Don't play games Dhanvita!"

"Well, they are interesting! Now I must read. Leave me alone!"

Shivani came to her thought pool after Dhanvita went. How can she find a guy who has spoken with her? What sort of a dumb clue was that? Nearly as much as guys from C.B.W. has spoken to her once in a while! But who'd that be? Who came and spoke to her that loves her? Days passed, Curios on the person Dhanvita had referred, Shivani spent a lot of time with her in the library asking again and again for who that person was. One fine Wednesday, Shivani and Dhanvita were sitting at a round table in the Library. Suddenly, our boy Surya had entered! Surya never ever stepped into library before in all of his days in C.B.W. He always asked permission to the librarian to go to the grounds at these periods, who was liberal to let him play.

That day, Surya had come to the library to take a chemistry guide for his nearing exams. Suddenly he saw Shivani. He was amazed! He noticed her sitting facing away from him. She couldn't see him. Surya cleared his throat to give a signal of his presence but Shivani was thinking about something else deeply that she didn't even hear his signal. Surya recognised she didn't turn and started to search for the book. By that way at least he could make her see him, by somehow falling in the range of her sight. He tried placing the books hard in their places, stomping the foot harder with his walks, clearing his throat again and again and coughing occasionally. But none of them worked. So, he finally went to get the book and leave.

Shivani got rid of the thought finally. She was exhausted on thinking who the person was. She stopped thinking and looked around to get hold of her physical presence. She only by then saw Surya! Surya tried everything before to get a glimpse of Shivani looking at him. But, he failed at that time. When she now looked, the unlucky chap was searching for his chemistry guide! Shivani, on seeing him, remembered the day when Surya had asked about the librarian. She was actually for the first time, was excited on thinking of the question "Is he the one?" She immediately started pulling Dhanvita's hand restlessly to call her. Dhanvita, who was first severely disturbed from her concentration hissed and turned back at Shivani. Both of their fast actions and sounds made Surya see them. For the first time, he saw the one next to Shivani, and happily found that it was Dhanvita. Surya immediately looked at Shivani's face and recognised her talks through her lips. She said.

"Hey! Even this guy spoke to me! Is he the guy? Is he the guy?" Shivani asked Dhanvita with a very much excited look; a look that's expecting the answer 'yes'.

Dhanvita turned back. She saw Surya. She was shocked to find him while she was with Shivani. Her plans would shatter if these two meet together. She immediately turned back to Shivani. Surya encountered all these clearly. When the girls found out Surya's seeing them, they fell silent. Surya couldn't believe his luck. He felt that something's going on with Shivani about him. He wanted to speak with Dhanvita later, to know what that was. He knew Dhanvita won't speak when she's with Shivani. So, he quietly went out of the library taking the book he found. He faced the open sky in the garden, and said,

"Thank God, I didn't understand chemistry!" and left.

Shivani's reaction on seeing Surya disturbed Dhanvita. Dhanvita was confused on how much he would have impressed Shivani already, for she wanted the answer to be him so badly. She kept quiet till Shivani wanted to leave. After the moment rose, both Shivani and Dhanvita started packing their bags to leave. When they came out, Dhanvita asked,

"What just happened there?"

"Nothing..." Shivani said with a naughty smile.

"Come on! Why did you shake me that much??"

"No, Dhaanu, you told me the clue that, it was a guy who spoke with me right? Even that boy spoke to me! That's why I asked you!"

"Asked??? You nearly were washing me like a cloth!"

"Chill girl... So, tell me, was he the guy?"

"What makes you think so?"

"He spoke with me too!"

"A lot of people did! Why is he so special?"

"Remember? You told me that it was the guy you hated! You tried to show him through the windows of 9th D! I saw this boy in that class too! That's why!"

"He was there? Are you sure?"

"YES! I am! I told you a boy was reciting the lessons right?"

"...The guy who made you speech-less?"

"I've told you! He was not the reason!"

"Ok, continue..."

"THIS was the guy who was RECITING!"

"WHAT!!!!!" Dhanvita screeched. What she thought before was now extremely wrong. Her assumptions were now upside-down! The guy who made Shivani speechless and the guy who's not even worth Shivani's slight look are same?? She thought to herself, "Why do these girls always try to fall into wrong hands? Why can't they just decide from a boy who'd treat them like queen? Why do they always choose to serve than be served? Now my task looks big! I must make Shivani hate Surya! It was a journey from Zero to full negative before, but now it is from full positive to full negative!" Dhanvita clearly understood that what Shivani told about the things that she claimed as reasons for speechlessness was a fake. She indeed was speech-less. But the bitter part was the guy being Surya!

Dhanvita cannot be stopped. Her misunderstanding with Surya grew day by day that saw no end. She engaged herself with her personal views in judging Surya and never even wanted to understand the truth! She was not that matured to analyse and realise the true nature of Surya. The matter of Surya's tease was just a matter of five percent anger in Dhanvita. Her anger was more influenced by the love he had in Shivani. Dhanvita's thoughts may seem stupid, but they're not unreal. Biggest failures in life happen due to small *feelings. In real life, haven't we encountered suicides committed by students who had failed or obtained low marks in the board exams or any other qualifying exams? It may be reasoned out as pressure, but it will lead to the simple feeling called fright. In our case, the simple misunderstanding left Dhanvita to do what she's doing now.*

"Yes Dhaanu, He was the one reciting." Shivani said.

"Well, you may like him, but he is not the one who said it."

"I don't like him, I just asked!"

"Can we stop this?? I hate these talks! Seriously please stop asking me questions!"

"Alright! Cool! Control your emotions! Let's go." Shivani said.

Both the girls walked together later. They never spoke about this topic again. But sure, Surya and Dhanvita knew that they would speak about this again. Though Shivani and Dhanvita spoke with each other, a separate part of Dhanvita's brain was thinking on what to say Surya that evening where he'd surely ask to what has happened in the library after he left.

Chapter 16: Link is broken.

"*That's it Surya! I told you everything! Even if you ask a million times it's the same!*" Dhanvita pleaded Surya. Surya was asking Dhanvita about what happened in the library again and again. Though Dhanvita told the whole thing Surya was not compromised. He too thought that there was something in Shivani's eyes when it came to Surya.

"Look, Dhanvita, you know how important it is to me. Just one more time! PLEEEEEAASSSEEEEE!!!" Surya begged.

"Alright, I've told Shivani that a friend of mine loves her, and that was the friend who teased me before."

"Oh, I'm sorry, but why did you tell about the fight to her? She'd misunderstand me to be rude!"

"Do you want me to continue or not?"

"Ok continue."

"Then she asked me for clues for who that was. I told her that it was a boy who came to her and spoke. That's it!"

"So, she still remembers my talk! WOW!!"

"Yes, so, when she saw you she asked me if that was you that's it."

"*But she looked excited!*"

"*She was excited for nearly all of her guesses.*"

"*So, when she guessed, what did you say?*"

"*I said no!*"

"*Thank God! Yes!!!*"

"*You're happy that I hid it?*"

"*Yeah*"

"*Why?*"

"*I should be the only one who should propose her!*"

"*Yeah, yeah buzz off!*" Dhanvita came off the topic and started leaving to the badminton court. Surya had been speaking with Dhanvita for nearly fifty minutes near the lawn outside of the badminton court. Now, after the discussion, Dhanvita went to watch her friends play. Surya was still standing in the place where she had left him. He was still imagining the looks Shivani gave on the library. Suddenly,

"*Surya?*" Dhanvita called. "*Want to see Shiv's handwriting?*"

"*What! You have her handwriting?*"

"*Yes, in a paper, I wanted to show you her handwriting, so I told her to write down the lyrics of "Chammak-Challo" to you!*"

"*You told that it was for me?*"

"*Obviously, no.*"

"*Good! Now come on show me!*"

Dhanvita went in the court. Surya came in a while later. Dhanvita took a crushed paper that was in her purse. It was a four-ruled paper, which children of primary schools used to practise their handwriting. She handed over the paper to Surya. Surya opened it straight and saw it and he was shocked. The handwriting was so... very... horrible!

"*What the hell!!*" *Surya exclaimed.*

"*What?*" *Dhanvita asked, puzzled.*

"*This can't be Shivani's handwriting. Stop fooling around. Take this and give it back to the kid you got it from!*" *Surya handed over the paper to Dhanvita and walked away.*

"*Even if you believe it or not that is Shivani's handwriting!*"

"*I won't believe!*" *Surya walked away.*

"*Then it's your wish.*"

Surya turned back. He didn't want to believe, but she was strong. Yet he again went back and got the paper. Saw the handwriting and sighed and said. "I don't know if you're telling the truth, but, if its Shivani's handwriting really, can I have that paper?"

"*Eww, What are you saying?*"

"*I just want to have it!*"

"Alright, have it... here." Dhanvita handed over the paper. Surya took it and kept it in his pocket. He was seeing the paper again and again later. Somehow he felt that it was not Shivani's handwriting, not because of logic, but also from his heart. Something repelled him. So, though he was said that it was hers, he couldn't believe it. While they were leaving the court, Surya finally gave a look at the paper. He only said, "It's not hers..." and threw the paper. Dhanvita saw him do that.

"What are you doing?" Dhanvita asked, shocked.

"That's not hers!" Surya replied.

"You're saying that I'm lying?"

"No, but I'm not having a feeling that it was hers."

"Whatever! Get lost." Dhanvita wanted to get rid of the talks. She was angry. Angry that Surya didn't believe in what she said. Well, she later was a little amazed. That indeed was not Shivani's handwriting. She did give a child's handwriting. It was one of her ideas for making Surya to know Shivani was not a big deal, not an angel that Surya's been fantasizing about and to know that she was no different from any other girl. When he realises, he would eventually lose his interest on her was her plan. But, did Surya have only interest on Shivani? What he had, though most may say as infatuation or crush, but pure true love, which would never decrease its level. Dhanvita was truly amazed on how Surya left over the paper she had given him. It was then Dhanvita found out that, there's no way that she can make Surya

forget Shivani… So she turned all of her focus back to Shivani in hating Surya.

It was the playground of C.B.W. The school had maintained the ground in a way that it was a Soccer ground in the centre, few trees towards its right viewed from the school's entrance and towards the left were the volleyball court and a handball court. Shivani, Dhanvita and few of Shivani's friends were talking. The next day was a holiday for the Republic day celebrations conducted by the school and I.E.C. So, to rehearse for those celebrations, the ground was now occupied by nearly three-fourth of the whole students of the school.

The performance that's going to be colourful the next day is now being crafted with the dust created through the children's movements. It's nearly a day-off for the school's normal functions. No classes were conducted, no teacher to ask for home-work, to keep test or to scold. So, every student was enjoying a holiday, at school itself. This was

the time when Dhanvita, Shivani and her friends sat in a step in the school ground that's joining the volley ball court to the soccer ground which was comparatively lower to the ground.

"Dhanvita, you brought your mobile!" A girl asked in shock.

"Yes… It's boring guys; no one will anyway ask either!"

"You've got guts girl!"

"So, what're you doing now Dhanvita?" Shivani asked.

"Texting…"

"With?" Shivani asked again.

"Why do you want to know?" Dhanvita teased.

"Just for general knowledge… Come on you twerp! Give me that!" Saying this, Shivani took Dhanvita's phone and started reading the texts. Dhanvita didn't stop Shivani. Anyway, it's actually what Dhanvita has planned.

"A message from… Surya… Hey alright Dhaanu, missing you here dear… Anyway! Why are you still in school darling? We're already playing here. Come soon…! It's no fun without you!" Shivani read this message and laughed, She thought Dhanvita had an affair, that too this soon. She continued to Dhanvita in a serious note…

"What is this message huh??? Dear??? Do you know what you're doing Dhaanu?"

"Oh I know what I'm doing... I'm not in any sort of relationship okay? It's this guy that's texting like this." Dhanvita said.

"He's texting like a real flirt!" A girl next to Shivani said.

"Yeah! A lot!!!" confirmed Shivani and asked, "Who's this Surya Dhaanu?"

"He's the guy whom you guessed in the library Shivani. Remember? He's the one whom I used to scold."

"What?!" Shivani asked, shocked.

"You seemed to be surprised?" Dhanvita asked.

"No, I'm not... it's just that I saw him that's all... I didn't know you got this much closer to him..." Shivani said in a low note. She's real serious now. She felt cheated. She didn't know what's happening around her. She nearly figured out that it was Surya who had told Dhanvita about loving Shivani. She realised from the behaviour of Surya and Dhanvita and their new friendship from the Palar Club. Whenever Surya did something crazy before Shivani, that she noticed and immediately Dhanvita talking about a similar incident and also her recent talks that were mainly concentrated on Surya, which made her come to the conclusion of the boy being Surya. Shivani was also impressed on the crazy things Surya did, things which were new to Shivani, making her interested in him, even without knowing his name.

With all these feelings, Shivani felt special. She experienced the feeling of being loved; a thing that became surprising was that, she too liked the feeling. So, when she just thought that someone likes her whole-heartedly she felt a little happiness. It can't be stated as a crush or love on Surya either. It's a normal simple happiness every human being will have. Won't we all be happy if a small baby feels comfortable with us, which laughs on seeing us, which would always choose our stretched arms in a group? Could we express it as love between a man and a woman? No. Well this is the same feeling Shivani experienced; but she herself thought at sometimes that it was crush on Surya and wondered why she felt so.

All these thoughts haunted Shivani for the past few days. That moment when she saw Surya on the library, searching for the book in the racks, she did feel something special. She did feel comfortable when she came to a fact that it could be Surya who loved her. It's compared to the sprouting of a small seed which when let to grow, would grow into huge, wide and would cast upon a shadow in the land for hundreds of years. The irony here is that, we live in an era, where trees are abolished from within the seed itself, which is the same thing that's now happening to Shivani. Dhanvita is now going to cut out the small sprouting seed with the knife; unlike a doctor's knife, but a cruel killer's, which wouldn't be gentle and is sure to leave a scar.

"Why the serious tone Shiv?" Dhanvita asked.

"No, I'm not becoming serious!" Shivani said, looking away from the phone.

"Girls, can you excuse us?" Dhanvita said to the other girls, present there.

"Why do we have to?" The girls quizzed.

"No, guys, it's not about speaking personal stuff. Just that we'll be speaking about the people only we know. You guys would feel bored right? That's why…" Dhanvita explained to the girls. They, on hearing this started to leave. Suddenly,

"NO! STAY!" Shivani raised her voice.

"What Shiv?" Dhanvita asked

"I don't know any Surya! It's your friend! Not mine! I don't know how do you even stay, but I won't even speak with any of my friends who are as flirty as this!"

"Shivani, why are you angry now?" Dhanvita asked. She felt her plan working.

"Why am I angry?? I'm seriously too much off the limits now! What's this guy thinking? Huh??? I seriously hate this message."

"Shiv… Shiv..! Stay! What's happened into you! Whoa, you haven't even seen the other messages! You've texted me using 'dear' right? I see no mistake here!?"

"It's no mistake for us speaking like that! We generally are brought up speaking that way with each other! But if you have been speaking like that with a boy! It's seriously Goddamn wrong!" Shivani was nearly

shouting at Dhanvita. She was angry on Surya a lot. She continued,
"And what do you mean by saying you haven't seen my other texts?"

"I don't know if I can say that... You're already tempered!" Dhanvita
fished for Shivani's anger and for her uncontrollable state.

"There's no hiding anymore. Anyway we've seen your messages already.
Now show us to the full." Shivani fell for Dhanvita's bait.

The conversation named-'Surya' was this:

Surya: Hey Dhaanu!! Where are you darling! ♥ ♥

Me: I'm in the grounds, with Shivani and her friends. ☺

Surya: Shivani! Ha-ha... Ok... Ok! Okay dear, when are you coming to the club darl?

Me: Why exclamation for Shivani?

Surya: As if you don't know babe. ;)

Me: Alright...

Surya: Dear, you know, I must speak to her one day!

Me: Why is that?

Surya: Just for fun darling! It is boring to speak only with a few people. We must get to know everyone. Right?

Me: She is much too occupied for that!

Surya: I bet I can make her speak!

Me: Well, best of luck with that task;

Surya: Ok, anyways dear, I will do it do not worry!

Me: Hmmm…

―――――――――――――――――

Then Shivani saw the final message that she had already read.

Surya: Hey alright… Dhaanu, missing you here dear… Anyway! Why are you still in school darling? We're already playing here. Come soon…! It's no fun without you!

"Too bad… Too bad Dhanvita! Don't ever speak with me about all this again and again. If you even say my name to him again, I will cut your throat off! Remember!" Shivani was boiling red. She was now in the uncontrollable and easy to influence state that Dhanvita baited for.

"Hey, I've never seen you this angry Shiv!" Dhanvita was really shocked. She could sense her success of the plan, Yet, she didn't knew Shivani could become this angry.

"Yeah? Why the hell have you been speaking about me with him? And what does he mean by, "Shivani, Ha-ha... ok ok!?" What does that mean?" Shivani asked.

"Guys, we really have to go! You guys talk, we'll be right back." The other girls who were hearing all this now felt that all of the talks were getting personal and withdrew themselves. But Shivani didn't leave them.

"We both know why you're going. Nothing's getting personal in here. Can you just sit?" Shivani ordered and continued, "Tell me, what it means!"

"Well, I'm sorry I lied to you Shivani, Well, it was Surya who had told me that he's in love with you." Dhanvita apologised.

"I know!"

"You did?" Dhanvita was shocked! She for a moment thought that Surya had already spoke much more to Shivani already and Surya had told his feelings to her. Dhanvita continued with confusion. "How?"

"I could guess it all from the behaviour of you and him with me!"

"Has he spoken to you?"

"NO."

"But..?"

"Look, all his actions and your stories of the boy who loves me? All leads to this okay! For the first time I'm regretting to have a friend like you! How can you tolerate to speak with a guy, who's this flirty huh?" Shivani was nearly shouting.

"Look Shivani it's not how it looks!" Dhanvita was a little startled. The course she set out was turned away from her plans.

"This is exactly how it looks!" Shivani threw back the phone to her and stood up to walk away.

"Shivani wait! Look, I know you'd understand me if you listen to me okay!" Shivani didn't care what Dhanvita spoke. She was walking away furiously. She was as angry on Dhanvita as much as she is with Surya. Though Surya texted like a flirt, Dhanvita let him speak so, without any objections was her anger's cause. Shivani was irritated on the cheap nature of her trusted friend. She was now merely a simple and immature minded fellow was Shivani's thought on Dhanvita. She never wanted to hear about Surya as well as Dhanvita too. Recognising this, Dhanvita was pushing her mind hard to come up with something that would make Shivani not to hate Dhanvita. Finally she did come up with the right words.

"Shivani… I told him a thousand times!" Dhanvita said in a high voice. Shivani stopped to hear it. Dhanvita continued. "I told him a thousand times to leave you and find another girl. He made me believe that he was truly in love with you. That's why I told him that I could help him to speak with you!" Dhanvita noticed that Shivani turned back. The anger didn't decrease; it increased even more on hearing those words. She came near Dhanvita and started to tell something, but Dhanvita intervened signalling Shivani to stop telling what she was about to tell, and continued.

"I recently recognised that he too was a fake and all he wanted was to make you love him, so that he could show off to people that he is in a relationship with the most beautiful girl in the school. When I understood this, it was the time I decided to help in making him not to speak with you. To help… you! I've tried so many times without your knowledge for resisting him in speaking with you. It's the reason that he has never spoke with you till now." Dhanvita caught Shivani's expression change. She continued, "The recent days, he's bugging me for making you speak with him. I was continuously resisting. He wanted to get into that topic today too. When I said I was with you, He said he will speak with you right? He's still determined on speaking with you. But, you yourself saw the reason, which he himself said. He's bored on talking with us and now he wants a new friend. That's all. That's why I tried to discourage him and wanted to make him stop. Now can you understand me? Or are you going to compare me with that rubbish and would leave me? But even if you leave me, I will still try to help you, in making him not coming to you!" Dhanvita finally finished her speech. She let this out with like a goods train that's coming out from the mouth of a tunnel. Fast, rumbling and sounds of air at times for the sake of breath.

"Are you serious about all this stuff Dhanvita? Are you telling the truth?" Shivani asked.

"Yes Shivani! One-hundred per cent I'm telling the truth!" Dhanvita swore.

"Then, why did you come up with love topics to me? Before, in the library, and why were you giving me clues to find out Surya? Than straight away tell it's him and not to near him?"

"Well, I was about to tell you in the library when you saw him that day! The day when you told me that he was the guy you saw reciting! But that day, you were pretty excited to know that it was him. I found it strange. I didn't know whether you spoke to him already and just that you wanted to confirm the fact of his love towards you was true or not. That's why I postponed in telling the matter to you at the right time. But after knowing that you haven't spoken to him, I wanted to tell you now. And that's why I've told you today."

"I know I over-reacted that day. Let's leave that topic. Now that I've known its Surya and now that I've known him clearly, there's no way that I'm going to speak with him, or see him ever again! I would make sure that even the air he breathes, the shadow he casts, the voice he lets out and the slightest influence of him would never even REACH me!!! You go and tell this clearly to him. Tell him that I'm not a fancy toy that he can use to show off and get a good name! I will be the person he'll never even dare to see if he speaks with me once!"

"Alright, calm down Shivani! I'll tell him, you don't worry, I will take care in finishing this!" Dhanvita said to Shivani. Well, to her, *she already finished the task she had. Surya would now never even have the chance in creating a good impression on Shivani. Shivani is now going to be long lost and never to be found in the life of Surya.*

Won't we all know Surya? We knew Surya was not careless about Shivani. Shivani was Surya's prized possession. She was the person Surya considered to be precious! Surya also, was a gentle and an honest boy from his birth. He was raised that way by his mom, dad and Hari too. Surya never took advantage on things that he had. He never got things that he wanted either. So, all he had, was to play with all that he has got, which made him gentle over the years in accepting the fact that, he's got what he needed. We all know Surya loved his friends. He loved Krishna, Varun, Preethi, Divya, Akansha, Neha and Dhanvita too. But he would never, ever, take them as an advantage. He really loves his friends, yet, He would know his limits with friends in the society. Surya would never call his friends by Dear, darling or honey. However close they may be. Well, Then you might ask, who was the one texting. Well, it was Divya.

Dhanvita's plan was to portray a flirt's image on Surya. It's what Shivani hates most on boys. She thought for so many days on how to do the act and when suddenly one day, Divya texted Dhanvita: 'What's up babe?' Dhanvita got the idea she was longing for. Girls usually text with themselves using the words 'dear, babe' which is just as normal as any other word in the girl-girl speech dictionary. Whereas it's completely wrong if that's a boy-girl speech dictionary, unless they're in love. When Dhanvita finally had a clear idea, she just waited for the right time to carry out her task. That opportune moment was the day before the republic day. Dhanvita was actually with Shivani beyond school hours. It was nearly 4:27, whereas school usually ends at 3:50. So, the situation was that, Divya and Preethi were already in the badminton court at PC. Hence Divya when bored, texted Dhanvita in the way we saw. Dhanvita just stored Divya's contact, in the name of Surya and was texting purposely to tempt Shivani guess what she was up to.

You may ask, what's with the text where Divya says, "Shivani... Ha-ha... I must speak with her". That's because, except Dhanvita no one has ever spoken to Shivani among the friends of Surya. With all those impressions Surya had created about Shivani among the friends, they always came up with 'speaking with Shivani' talks, Just to have a simple laugh on Surya's famous dialogue,

"I must speak with Shivani, no matter what!"

That was the reason Divya too said that way in her texts, which, Dhanvita's mind had used effectively.

Chapter 17: Realising disappointment.

*I*t was the 26th of January, 2011, The Indian republic day. The place where Surya's father worked was a central government company, which provided schooling facilities and an extra-ordinarily well-kept township. It was in this place that schooling of two syllabuses, one offered by the CBSE and the other offered by the state government, two clubs, a giant soccer ground that was in control of the clubs, rather than the similar, yet smaller ground maintained by the schools, well developed shops, and temples, mosque and a church was also kept. All maintained and funded by the company.

This company had maintained celebrations for various government holidays and festival days. They celebrated the Independence Day, the Republic day, New Year, May Day etc. Usually the Independence and Republic day were the stars of these celebrations. This day, was the Republic day, the star celebration in the just started year.

Remember the long road that Surya walked in sadly, few days before? The roads were cold and damp that day. But this day, it's fresh! It's been severely decorated with lots of balloons and flags with the colours, saffron, white and green, depicting the Indian tri-coloured flag. That day, Surya walked alone. He was only accompanied by a sad, cold wind. But now, the places were filled with people. Everyone was making their way to the podium in the soccer ground's bottom most ends. That was the place made for people to sit and enjoy the performances that will happen during these celebrations.

The celebration was always started with the chief-guest's speech, which was mostly about India, Then followed by the March past event conducted by both the schools joined together, later, cultural competitions would start in order, where children of kindergarten and primary schools join to perform on patriotic songs. Later, the senior students' dance from any of the schools and a group activity, based on stunts, or aerobics would continue till the end of the celebrations with the Indian National Anthem.

Now, the time was already 8:30 a.m. The flag was hoisted, salutes made, march past parade was now ended too. It's the time of cultural feast of the dance made by the kindergarteners. Though they rarely made mistakes occasionally, people were enjoying it. Their performance was so cute, that their mistakes were always forgiven and forgotten. While these people dancing, and the whole crowd cheering them up, a group of people were seriously involved over some issue. They were concentrating on another group in the very same crowd, who were also enjoying the performances.

"Come on! Send the message! Dhanvita will show it to her!" Krishna said.

"Man, you know about me…" Our boy Surya said.

"... and that's why I'm not going to ask you anymore. Give me that!" Saying this, Krishna pulled out the mobile from Surya's hands, typed a text furiously to Dhanvita and handed over the phone to Surya.

"What did you send?" Surya asked.

"I want to speak with Shivani. Show her this message and ask her if she can do it!" Krishna spoke out of what he had sent while Surya was reading it.

"WHAT!" Surya exclaimed.

"Look! Clearly all of us are bored with your state. When the hell are you going to speak? You could speak on 30th of February. But I can't wait that long!" Krishna said.

"30th? In February?" Divya asked.

"Yes! Have you ever saw a 30th in February?" Krishna said.

"No..." Divya replied.

"Obviously" Preethi added.

"Precisely!" Krishna finished.

"I can't understand?!" Akansha asked, puzzled.

"Look, if I say like that, it means Surya's never going to speak! Understood that you tube-lights?" Krishna said.

"Enough! All of you! Look Dhanvita is showing the phone to Shivani!" Surya said. When he said that, all the people of the gang, saw the *other gang members who were seated below in the first two rows of the podium. Whereas Surya and his friends were seated in the higher deck, nearly second row from the top of the podium. Dhanvita decided to stay with Shivani. Her plot is now entering to the end.*

"Shivani's seeing!" *Surya screeched in excitement.*

"She didn't reply! She turned back to see the dance!" *Krishna exclaimed.*

"Ask Dhanvita what happened!"

"Yea, I'm texting now!" *after a few minutes,* "Dude, She didn't tell anything to Dhanvita either." *Krishna said.*

"Ohhh!!!!!!!!!!" *Surya sounded in expressing his anger.*

"Wait! Here's a text from Shivani herself from Dhanvita's number!" *Krishna said. At once, Surya picked the phone from him and read the message. It said:*

"If you really have the guts, come and speak with me! —Shivani"

"Whoa… a sudden twist in the story!" *Krishna said.*

"Great!" *Surya said.*

"Are you going to go Surya?" *Akansha asked.*

"Of course! She's asked about my guts! Can't lose it!" *Surya said.*

"You Sure?" *Preethi asked.*

"YES!"

"That's my friend!" Krishna said.

"Text her back that I will meet her as soon as the function gets over!" Surya said.

"YES!" Krishna replied.

"Things are becoming good!" Surya said.

"Done bro... Get ready!"

From that moment! Surya didn't see the performances. He practised on what he has to speak with Shivani. He came up with good phrases that he himself loved to say. Everyone helped him too. Then, by 10:45, the functions came to an end. Shivani's friends started to leave. They sat in the bottom, which made them come out of the podium and leave it quickly. While, Surya delayed for a time interval of five minutes to even get off the podium's stairs. When Surya and his friends finally got down, Surya saw that Shivani and her friends were already so far away from the ground. Surya saw Dhanvita coming to them. But he didn't have the time to speak with Dhanvita. So he started running, bidding bye to the people present with him. They too, wished Surya luck. Surya ran away from his friends, from the podium, from the ground to the parking lot where he had kept his father's bike. He took it and started it and raised the throttle to the full limit. He released the clutch and accelerated so fast that the wheel had skidded and started to move. Surya controlled the bike and set course to speak with

Shivani. Shivani was walking on the other side of the road. So, Surya went past her and took a turn and came back.

Shivani saw these. She understood that Surya is now here to speak. She didn't expect him to come and speak, but Surya is now coming back. Surya came behind Shivani and parked the vehicle in the road, and started following Shivani from behind by foot. Shivani's friends were looking at Surya again and again and told Shivani that Surya was coming. Shivani wanted to avoid him and started walking fast. When a girl saw Surya, he told her to call Shivani. As he told, the girl called Shivani. Shivani on realising there's no hope anymore, turned back and came to Surya. Finally, for real, the first real talk between Surya and Shivani happened.

"H... HI..." Surya said. Shivani didn't reply. Surya couldn't wait. He started speaking.

"You accept that I've got guts now? You said that if I had got guts I will have to come and speak to you right? Job is done." Surya said.

"It wasn't me. It was my friends. I didn't send it." Shivani said, looking at the ground.

"Oh, well anyway, we've spoke... Do you..." Shivani interrupted when Surya was talking.

"Look, I'm not interested in speaking with you... I'm not interested in anything." Shivani said.

"I just want to be a friend with you Shivani!" Surya said. He was shocked.

"I'm not interested in anything! NO!" Shivani said.

"Why?" Surya asked.

"I am just not interested in being even a friend with you." Shivani said.

"You never know me Shivani! You're deciding too fast. First let's know..." Shivani again interrupted.

"I've known you enough. I've seen your texts. I know what feeling you have with me."

"You know?" Surya asked.

"Yes. And now let me be really clear. I would never ever want to have even a little drop of friendship with you understand? And if you could do me a real favour, please do not make me see you again!" Shivani said firmly. Surya couldn't speak. He thought Shivani has now already known the fact of his love towards her but she hasn't felt his love towards her. He felt that there's nothing to say anymore. He just said bye to her and stood. Shivani didn't say anything. She just went after Surya said bye and never turned back. Surya stood there for a while. Surya had finally spoken with Shivani. His dream has come true. Well, was that his dream? Was this what he wanted to be special? Was this his love's reward? Why did things that a young boy wants so badly are just taken away as simple as that? What happened to the things that he imagined? Why doesn't life just be beautiful as

the mind visualizes? What happiness does God get by making his lovers feel cheated? Was his longing too much for one to have, that it had to be taken away?

These were the questions that lingered in Surya's mind. Surya couldn't understand what had just happened to him. His world of happiness was now broken down in an instant. Surya felt as if he was being shot. Every time Surya saw Shivani, she shot bullets of happiness in his heart that would explode into magic glitters inside the body when reached and that would spread like fire as if it was fuelled. Even now, she shot at Surya. Those bullets reached his body. It knocked him out clearly as before. But only now, it gave him pain. He felt hurt. He felt the pain clearly. Something from within knocked his throat, trying to burst out of his chest. His poor heart, just hand sized, wanted to pump harder, as if it was the only way to pump out the pain, but then, later, his mind decided to stop. But, even the mind couldn't control his heart. Seeing all this confusions from within, the eye, didn't do anything, but cried.

Tears came oozing through those eyes, which were just so happy moments ago. Visions blocked, mind heated, heart cold, damp and heavy, Surya closed his eyes, trying to feel her aroma, hear her voice, to see her eyes in the simple tool of imagination. But, his mind resisted, he came back to reality, to what he thought once was his, and now gone, forever and far away. Realising this, his heart bled. His soul had burnt before in seeing her... in happiness. It laughed by then, but now, when it burnt, it mourned deeply. His soft and tender soul was crushed, smashed, beaten and burnt. There were no more words that could signify the sorrow he felt.

Surya felt everything he had in him that signified his life drained out. He didn't feel his heartbeat... he couldn't feel the air that's trying to console him, by caressing him on its way... He saw a flower in bush nearby him. It was dangling with the air, like a bell jiggling. Surya thought, "Poor guy, being shook by someone for no cause, just with an intention of play." What Surya meant clearly defined his feeling. If Surya had seen this view before, he would've said, "He's so happy that he's dancing his way out of his plant."

Well, Surya knew one thing. He couldn't make Shivani love him in compulsion. That couldn't make love last forever truly. The only way one can make a girl love, is to share his love. Not through compulsion, not through crazy acts, but just to show his feeling open heartedly. Well, what happened now was that his love can't be shown now, not anymore either. She went away from him, telling him not to follow, not to come back. He couldn't hurt her. He just wanted to follow what she has said. His Shivani is now gone. Well, she's not 'his' Shivani anymore too. Surya could've tried, but he didn't want to. He just wanted Shivani to be happy. He doesn't want him to become the reason for even a simple irritation in Shivani's heart. His path was now clear. It's a dead end. No further way possible. Even Surya realised it.

He just faced the sky and talked to the only one who knows everything. "Why don't you just give what I want? If you don't want to give me something, better don't show them to me! Why do you show me something, make me imagine having it, and why do you take it away!" Well, he knew there won't be any reply. He just shook his head in disappointment and took his dad's bike and started leaving the place. He once glanced at the place that he had spoken with Shivani and thought, "The most heavenly place, which did a hell's job." and sighed deep.

What he didn't know was that, Shivani too, sighed deep on leaving the place. It was not her intention to object Surya's request. All she knew was that, Surya never felt Shivani special. To her, all she knew about Surya's intentions were just to show off, which was the only reason that made her angry on him. Also, the messages that Dhanvita showed, made her upset on Surya. Shivani thought, she had experienced happiness on Surya's actions, her only regret was that, she has now ended up in a Fool's Paradise...

Chapter 18: Krya.

*T*hey say 'change alone is constant.' If there are days of winter, there is going to be a spring soon. If there are downs, there will be ups. Everything is balanced in this whole wide world. It is this balance that sustains life. Great kingdoms have fallen, kings defeated, monuments were crashed, but, they rise back up; people get to stay calm again, they can have their peace back.

The way Surya's love ended was a sad grief that Surya has to carry. It was his first love. He never figured out why Shivani couldn't understand him and why she had so much anger in him. Surya after that day went to his friends and told them what had happened. Dhanvita, hearing all that, put a lot of effort in making Surya forget Shivani. Later as days passed, she realised that she had no responsibility to do that. After all, her intention was not to make Surya forget Shivani. It's the other way round. So, she retreated to her old state with Surya. She never spoke much again as before. That day, Krishna, Preethi, Divya, Akansha and Neha, consoled Surya. They were full supportive to him. Surya went to the club only to see them and spend some time with them. His interest in badminton decreased too. Why should he play anymore? His competition was over, his passion was over and most of all, his Shivani was now not there to show off either.

After that incident, Surya saw Shivani rarely. She never came out of her class as before and he too didn't have the strength to speak with her again. Even if they had met occasionally, Surya would walk away. Days passed till the month of June the same way. Later, Surya got his tenth grade board exam results. He scored a grade point of 8.8/10. His intention was to continue in C.B.W. but, due to the shouting he got from his principal, in securing a bad grade from what the teachers had expected, Surya decided to change his school. He, of course didn't have his Shivani either. Surya never saw her after his exams. He thought that Shivani too, would've moved to any other school. He did know that she scored a grade point of 9.6/10. With that as a grade, she would've gone to any good schools, even away from the district. Thinking of that in mind, Surya left C.B.W., to have his higher secondary education in another school nearby. The school's name was Krya.

That was the second most famous school in the district. This school too, followed the same syllabus offered by CBSE. The school had the high-class students of the district. Than C.B.W., the infra-structure of this school is way better, costing a more sum of money from Surya's dad's pocket. The school obviously was costing a reasonable amount of fees, but due to the company's management in C.B.W, Surya's father had to pay only few sum of money as fees before. The school also had another building, which taught students the syllabus offered by the State Govt. There are three different groups of subjects, with which the students can choose, in both of these syllabuses. One, subjects concentrated on areas of Physics, Chemistry, Maths and Biology; two, concentrated on Physics, Chemistry, Computer Science and Maths and finally the subjects that offered commerce topics, like accounting, maths, etc.

Surya never had interests in accounts, and biology either. So, he chose the second group, which consisted computer science. He did know Krishna would leave him soon. Krishna opted for the syllabus offered by the state govt. for seeking better opportunity in getting an engineering seat in a good college inside Tamil Nadu. Surya didn't want to change his syllabus. Though he had good opportunity in getting into college, he refused changing due to the different evaluation processes undertaken in the state govt.'s syllabus. So, with all that in mind, Surya joined in Krya's CBSE School.

That was the first day in Krya…

The school's uniforms were not yet announced. They planned to do it during the first day's assembly, to ease out the announcing process. The Students were made to sit in their respective classes until they get a teacher to guide them to the assembly. Surya was now in his standard outfit. A t-shirt and a blue jeans and the big Fastrack watch at his right hand, holding the Cherokee bag that's hanging only to his right shoulder. He was walking from the entry gates, to the school's doors. He looked up the building. The school was built in every modern way it could hold. A semi-circular building, arena typed. In its middle, there was a garden, and the whole classrooms, arranged from left to right in the 3 storey building.

"That is a big school!" Surya said to himself.

He walked through the big doors, and searched for 11th grade classroom. He asked the receptionist for its location and had gone to it as per her instructions. Surya found the classroom, and found an empty seat at the first bench. He went and sat there. He was just sitting idle. He had no idea on what to do. He looked around the classroom. The classroom was filled with children, his fellow classmates. Surya saw each of them. At the very end of the classroom, he saw nearly fourteen boys, grouped together and talking out loud. Their sound dominated the whole classroom. He then, saw the benches before them. He saw many students, sitting as quiet as Surya. They didn't know what to speak anything either. Later he saw way beyond these benches, farther to the wall side. Those were the section of seats for the girls. He saw them too. He didn't think of anything in seeing them. He looked blank and turned to his row. He saw the bench just behind him empty. And the bench next to that was occupied by three students. They were speaking about some hilarious topic, that only they knew, which made the guy sitting in the middle laugh hysterically, making the bench shake, syncing to his body's shake. Surya saw those, and turned back. He thought, 'let's hope this shouldn't turn out like A.K.R.S.' Then suddenly someone tapped Surya by his shoulder. Surya turned to look who that is.

"Hi! I'm Komalesh! Don't ask me what it means, I don't know it either. Keep it Koma!" The boy came in and introduced himself to Surya.

"Oh… Hi Koma! I'm Surya." Surya replied. He now clearly saw the boy to whom he was talking with. Koma was a lean guy, who toned up his arms and legs, though when he didn't have any muscles to show-off. He wore on a loose red striped glittery shirt and a formal pant. The most attractive feature that he had was his whole head. His head was shaped like a China dish with a lid; a horizontal fat oval. He had both of his central incisors pointing out together, joined in the shape of the head of an arrow and a moustache that was trimmed only days ago.

"Surya… It's a really nice name! Where did you do your schooling Surya, till your tenth grade?" Koma asked.

"C.B.W."

"Where is that precisely?"

"What! You don't know C.B.W.?"

"Not a clue."

"My teachers had said that it was a gifted school, and that we were all gifted to get a seat in it! They even said that it was the most successful school in the district!" Surya exclaimed.

"Come on dude, that's what exactly my previous school had said before and expect this, even our teacher, from this school would say that!" Koma said.

"Alright. Anyway, what's your school's name?"

"R.M.D. ICSE School." Koma replied.

"Wow! ICSE? The International Curriculum of Secondary Education?"

"Yea! Don't exclaim for ICSE, it's just the Syllabus recognised even in other countries and nothing more."

"Why didn't you continue in that syllabus?"

"I couldn't withstand the pressure of that syllabus in the higher secondary! It gets tougher by then. Only the Smarty pants can stay there."

"Okay anyway, we're buddies from now on bro!"

"Cool man!"

"By the way, do you have any idea about who those guys at the back are?"

"*They are the guys who studied here from high school. I saw most of them during the admission procedures.*"

"*Oh, that's why they aren't looking as awkward as us!*"

"*Ha-ha! Yea man!*"

"*Good morning Students!*" Mrs Nancy entered the classroom rushing. She then continued, "*Students! Today's Monday, the first hour is mine, I'm Mrs Nancy, your chemistry teacher. Now, we'll continue our introductions after the assembly. Line up and go for the stage quietly and sit where your Physical education teachers instruct you to. Hurry up!*" Surya, Koma, and every other student who were present in the class went on as Nancy ma'am has said.

The assembly of Krya was as normal as every other assembly in every school. They started with a prayer, and a school song, with a talk from the teacher, an announcement and finally end with the school's song that focuses on the school and its motto. This was the first assembly of the year. So, this day, announcements held a more important place. The school's correspondent Mr Chandrasekhar greeted the students warmly. He started informing the students about the details of uniforms, the school's timing, the availability of buses etc. Later that day, after all the announcements, the school's senior most students gave a performance to cheer up the fresher of the school.

After the "*fresher's day celebrations*" in the assembly, students were sent to their respective classrooms. Surya and Koma went together to the class. When they reached the class, it was already 10:15 a.m.

They saw Mr Xavier already in his desk. They saw him and asked his permission to enter the class. After his agreement with that, they sat in their places quietly. Both of them were instantly captured by the cold figure of Mr Xavier.

Mr Xavier was the school's senior most Mathematics teacher. He was well-known for his voice. It was a cold, echoing bass voice. Students of that school were always scared of him. He was tall, skinny and long faced. He always wore a formal outfit, to be precise, each and every day it was a full sleeved striped-shirt, with a dark coloured pant. He'd keep it tucked in and the pant never went beyond his toes. His movements are always slow, as slow as a robot, which eventually was his nick-name that students kept. He speaks very less. Even now, when Surya and Koma had asked permission, he just nodded.

"Dude who's he?" Surya asked.

"As if I'm his relative…" Koma replied.

"Alright, ask Mr Smarty pants." Surya said, pointing to a guy sitting next to Koma.

"Hey pal… Who's that?" Koma asked the boy.

"He's Mr Xavier our maths teacher." The boy said.

"Ohhh… I'm Komalesh, and you are?" Koma asked.

"I'm Shankar." He replied.

"Ohhh… You're from this school?"

"Yup!"

"Okay! Thanks." Koma left out Shankar on that topic and continued with Surya. *"Look bro, He's our Maths teacher!"*

"What!!! Man, I don't have a good feeling about him."

"Why?"

"I just don't know."

By 10:30, Mr Xavier rose up. He was so tall that Surya and Koma, who were sitting on the first bench, looked up so high. After a pause, making the students look at him, Mr Xavier continued.

"Students, I'm Xavier, your Mathematics teacher. I'll be taking you this subject this year and the next year too. All I want to tell you is this. I'm a perfect teacher myself and I want all my students to be perfect too." Xavier told this in his very own, bass echoing voice. Surya and Koma frowned upon his statement. Mr Xavier continued...

"Today, I'll just give you an intro about what you're going to study this year. First, we'll start with the complex numbers and..." Mr Xavier told that he would take an introduction class of the lesson, which is, the first chapter itself. The class went on till 11:00. Five minutes past the break time. Everyone was exhausted after that. Koma and Surya got up and walked out of the class.

"Whoa... is he even a human being!?" Surya asked panting.

"I guess not!" Koma replied.

"Man! The meanest teachers I ever met in my earlier classes too left the first classes. Look at this guy! Oh my God!" Surya said.

"Me too bro, I've never seen such a villainy in anyone before!"

"I think it's going to be a very long two years of mathematics bro!" Surya exclaimed.

"Yea. I'm afraid that is so!"

After the class taken by Mr Xavier, the two friends had a break at 11:00 am to 11:05 till the next class. They decided on getting out, to the canteen. The boys' class was in the second floor and the canteen was in the ground floor, a few feet away from the school building. They climbed down the stairs, and went to the canteen. Surya was happy that his school had an exceptionally good place, for students to eat. In C.B.W. all that was given to the students was a samosa, which also, had to be achieved through a great struggle from the other students, with some teachers as well.

The boys went inside. Surya caught a good view of the canteen. It had a full brick designs in the interior and the exterior, a big place for students to sit and eat, and at the edge of the hall there had been the people who run that canteen. People who take out tokens from the students, which is nothing but the bill for the food that the student's had ordered, and give the food when prepared accordingly to them. In the very corner of that edge, there was a small section that only provides juices and beverages.

"So, what do you want to eat Surya?" Koma asked.

"Oh whatever you're having. I'm not in the mood to choose" Surya said.

"Alrighty, Lets have the samosas, ten bucks a pair. You okay with that Surya?"

"Yep, Fine." Surya said. Though all his years he had only tasted samosas, he still wanted to go by his friend's choice. He didn't want to disappoint him anyway.

"You go and sit there. I'll bring 'em." Koma said to Surya.

"Okay."

Surya was seeing around the canteen. His mind couldn't take it as a canteen. It was huge and was looking as rich as a hotel. Just while Surya was looking at it, He saw Koma coming by with the two pairs of Samosas. He came and sat next to Surya.

"Won't we be late? It's already 11:05." Surya asked.

"Why worry dude? It's the first day." Koma replied, while giving his samosa a 'bath' with ketchup.

"Yea, you saw the first day of Mr Xavier!"

"Oh-ho-ho! Yea man! The robot! God! Look at the nerve of some people!"

"Yes Koma, now I notice that you too didn't like that guy!"

"What do you mean?"

"Oh nothing, it's just that I saw a guy named Koma in the maths class telling the sir the answers of questions at every instant as a bullet. I thought that he liked the subject and his teacher and eventually the interest, towards solving problems."

"Ha-ha! Dude, you haven't understood me. It's not about telling answers, it's about performance! You got to have some reputations in the school bro!"

"Performance?" Surya chuckled.

"Yes sir!" Koma chuckled too.

"Great sir, I'll keep that in mind."

"Now, eat your samosas and let's go" Koma ordered and started to leave.

"Oh Mr Performance, Wait up!" Surya called. Koma laughed at this and sat again.

After Surya had finished eating, both of them started leaving the canteen and off they went to the class. While walking, Surya asked Koma...

"What do you think of these guys Koma?"

"Which guys?"

"All of them in our class."

"Hmm, I'll definitely say they're rich bro. Rich enough for not to study."

"Dude, I thought the same."

"What's your father Surya?"

"A deputy manager in I.E.C."

"Oh, my dad's the dealer for Pepsi, through-out the district."

"Seems like we're sailing in the same boat bro. Both of our families are middle class."

"Yup, No doubt in that…" Surya and Koma went to the class and saw no teacher. They just went and sat in their places. It was only Mr Xavier's that they are ship-wrecked for the two years. Other teachers were not as cruel as him. Some of them were so very kind, that they didn't even come to the class. Students were left free to talk, play and do whatever they wanted to.

Time passed and later came the lunch hour. Nothing special was there in that. Surya and Koma ate their food that was brought from home.

"New school… Mom's food! I'm so happy to have this time!" Surya said to Koma.

"Why that sentence now?"

"Nothing, My last episode of joining in a new school was a tragedy. I was made to join as a hosteller. I had severe home-sickness back then, where I cried and cried all day long, throughout the nights, during break-fast, lunch, dinner…"

"Surya stop! I get it, don't cry now okay! Whoa, what a cry baby you are!" Koma teased and continued, "I would have been much happier if I had joined in a boarding school."

"No you won't, you wouldn't know how cruel boarding schools are Koma."

"Oh man, you just didn't realise the enjoyment! I tell you boarding schools are the best in schooling if you'd ask me!"

"No Koma, it's as they say, you won't get to know the value of a thing unless we lose it. The time I lost my parents, was the time I have realised their true value."

"Maybe, you are true. But I just don't want to agree to that Surya!" Koma started arguing. It's his way of arguing about something that even if he loses the argument, he'd still continue arguing about the same topic from his side. He never accepted his failures. At times even doubts may arise, whether he had understood his failure or not. But his remarkable feature was that, he would make his points sound absolutely true, even if it was completely the other way round in real.

"Oh get lost bro!" Surya finally withdrew from the conversation.

The friends later changed topics about films, computers etc. Later, it was the end of the day. Surya and Koma were to board the buses that would make them reach their homes, to which Surya's dad had paid Rs. 3,500 per three months' term. Surya looked for his bus route. The school had a total of 20 buses for different routes that covered nearly 40kms around the school. Surya, as we know was 17kms away from school. His route was covered by buses namely 19 & 20. He could board any of them. The two friends started from bus 1, to find their buses. The bus that led Koma to his home was Bus no. 16. He found it out at first. He and Surya went inside it and Koma kept his bag in it and hopped out to find Surya's bus. Both friends had to walk again till they saw the sign board that read Surya's neighbourhood, I.E.C. campus. Finally both the friends saw no. 19 & 20. Surya went up at 19, kept his bag and came out. Both of them sat at a raised platform near the buses.

"So, what do you think will be happening in this school for these two years Koma?" Surya asked

"Because of us?" Koma asked, teasing.

"Ha-ha maybe... But my question was not because of us, but for us." Surya said, after both the friends, exchanged a laugh.

"Well, I think it would be good, and if it's not, let's make things turn good bro!" Koma said. Surya liked Koma's courage and his perspective of life. Surya always wanted to have this attitude. Well, some are born with these attitudes, some can acquire these attitudes and some are like Surya, always longing and never achieving.

As Surya and Koma were talking, Surya saw few girls walking by; he thought that he had recognised them, only later he had really came to know about whom those girls were. They were Surya's old school mates. Some are Surya's friends in that very same group.

"Look Koma, all of them are from my school!" Surya said. "I never knew these girls too had joined here."

"I don't think I've seen them today in our class Surya? And this looks like a real big herd!" Koma said.

"No bro. They might've chosen the state board syllabus."

"Hmmm... maybe."

The girls were talking loudly when they had walked towards Surya and Koma. They came that way because eventually, the girls of C.B.W. was also living in the same place that Surya had been living all these years. So, they too had to board the buses 19 or 20. Surya saw them board the bus 19. He cursed his luck. Most of the time he never liked the way girls of C.B.W. behaved. Generally none of them behaved well to him. Surya always felt jealousy, selfishness and lots and lots of attitude in their behaviour. So, he never had a good side in girls. It was only Shivani and some others were exempted from Surya's eyes. What caught Surya was, his childhood friends, the friends across the street, the people whom he had played street cricket and Shuttle throughout the summer of 2009, were in the crowd too. They were Nisha and Priyanka. Both of them saw Surya, but at that time Surya had been talking busily with Koma. And when Surya saw them, they were already boarding the bus.

"Man, see how these girls change!" Surya said to Koma.

"Huh? Why?" Koma asked.

"Gee, bro, I nearly spent my whole high school with the two girls in that herd, and since they've joined in a new school, I'm also a past memory… They didn't even see me!"

"Oh, come on! It's too soon to think like that! Well, I also accept, girls' changes occur but I think it's too soon bro."

"Don't you get it? I'm just an 8.8 pointer, and they're 10/10. What more explanation do you want?"

"Hmm, suits your statement bro… But…" The screeching whistle of the Physical Education teacher tore through Surya and Koma's ears, interrupting their talks. The teacher was now here to make sure all the children board their buses. Surya said,

"All right bro… See you tomorrow!" Surya bid bye.

"Yes dude!" saying that, Koma came to embrace Surya, to bid bye. Surya jolted back.

"Dude…! What're you doing?" Surya asked with a frowned face.

"Bidding bye?!" Koma asked, confused.

"NO! Not this way! Only girls do like this! Never ever bid bye to me like that alright!"

"Alright grumpy, good bye…" Koma just waved and walked to his bus.

Surya boarded his bus and sat in the fourth seating row from the front. While he was sitting, Surya heard a lot of loud voices from the back, which said "Hey come on tell him Priyanka!" "No, it's true, He

*doesn't know" "Come on, Priyanka! Tell!" "Priyanka!!!" "Priyanka!!"
Most of the time all that Surya heard was the name Priyanka, the
name of his friend. Surya didn't respond to those voices and was just
sitting. A moment later, Kavya, a girl from the gang, came up to
Surya and said,*

*"Hey, this bus is only for the girls from our area. Boys must board the
next bus." saying that, she just went back to her seat.*

*Surya didn't board the bus in the morning. Hari had dropped him
in the school and went. Surya believed Kavya and went down to the
second bus. Surya saw the last bus. Bus no. 20. The bus looked nearly
a thousand years old. It actually belonged to a museum, but some
miser, had put on some screws to it and is still working with it.*

*"Shit, where's humanity to boys!" Surya cursed the bus and started
boarding it. To his surprise, Surya found Nandhu in the bus. Nandhu
was Surya's classmate. He was a Kryan, from sixth grade. His mom
is a math teacher in Krya. Nandhu was a tall, very skinny guy, who
lived just a few Kilometres away from Surya's house. Surya saw him
and said...*

"Hey, bro... Good thing you're in this bus too!"

*"Hey... Where are you from Surya? Are you too in this bus?" Nandhu
asked*

"Yes dude, I'm from I.E.C., you?"

"I'm from Housing board bro... Just two stops away from your area!"

"Oh, that's great dude!"

"So, if you're in I.E.C., Why'd you board this bus Surya? The previous one also goes to the stop right?"

"Yes, but that's a girl's only it seems, only to my stop. That's why I boarded here bro."

"Bullshit! Who said you?"

"The girls in there…"

"They've tricked you bro, there's never any girls only or boys only stuff in the buses of our school!"

"What the HELL!!!!!!!!!!!!!"

"Now, calm down. Leave it. Anyway, they helped in letting us know each other!"

"Come on bro… She tricked me to come in this Goddamn dog catching van!"

"Ha-ha…"

"Goddamn Kavya!" Surya cursed.

The driver mounted in his seat, the bus started with a heavy shake. As shaky as a dog's body, that came from a swim. All its rusted seats and bars to hold on, every screws and nuts and nails that held the bus vibrated.

"*Earthquake's much better dude!*" *Surya said to Nandhu. Both of them shared a laugh.*

The bus started to leave the campus. The first bus to I.E.C. went before them, Surya watched it with hate. He saw the gang of girls that had made him a fool. To be precise, he was seeing Kavya as if his eyesight itself would burn her completely. He was later carried on with the travel, this was Surya's first school bus ride... all these 12 years, from his kindergarten to his tenth grade, he never went on buses, and he just enjoyed the experience though the bus was that old!

Later after the journey, first Nandhu departed from his stop with his mother. Surya bid bye to him, and he was ready to get down when his stop comes. After he got down, Surya walked to his home and shared the experiences of the new school's first day. Rather crying when in A.K.R.S., this time Surya loved sharing his feelings... with his family, happily.

Chapter 19: Farewell my friend...

"*So, That's it bro! That's the whole story of my first day at school!*" *Surya said.*

Surya and Krishna were sitting on a park bench in their neighbourhood. Surya had told everything about his first day at Krya. Surya also told the information of the event he had encountered with the bus, which Krishna told to forget. Both the friends sat on the bench, enjoying the mighty, beautiful sun's path way down to the ground. Surya and Krishna did nothing but enjoy the silent sunset. They were also tired, from a long, hard game of badminton. They had just bid bye to their friends Preethi, Akansha, Neha, Divya and Dhanvita, who too had a good game. Surya had also heard them saying that they won't be playing in PC anymore. They had to go to another court nearby which had a new paint, new nets, and new competitors with a new coach. They decided on improving their game and have thought to go for it.

Surya was worried. He didn't know what to say, they do have the interest in badminton yet. They deserve a good trainer. Who knows? They can be champions in this game too. Though heavy hearted, Surya said his friends a goodbye. Perhaps that was their last match in PC that they had played so well and hard that day. Surya didn't know what to feel anyway. His best chain was now broken. His family is now apart. He just wanted everything to be okay from now. His best moments may have been over. But no one knows what his moments will become. So, with anticipation, hope and a little grief he watched the sun.

"Shivani stayed." Krishna started.

"What?" Surya asked.

"Shivani stayed. She's continuing in C.B.W."

"Hmmm." Surya said, with his eyes concentrating only the sun.

"Do you trust me Surya?" Krishna asked suddenly.

"Yes."

"Then please answer me Surya! Why haven't you tried again?"

"It's not right Krishna!"

"Surya...! Come on! Every time I ask you this question you answered in one line. I want an explanation."

"Krishna, you won't understand it... Please stop!"

"Surya, I've grown with you for five years now. I can even know what you think. So shut up and say now!"

"Then why can't you hear what I think now?" Surya's voice nearly trembled. Krishna brought back the memories of Shivani's talks to Surya. His most prized possession said it doesn't need him. The most paining thing was that she didn't want Surya ever again. She hadn't given him a life sentence, but a death sentence. Surya couldn't tolerate to what he had been cast upon. The event was really a harsh memory for Surya. It's a young age, the age where he couldn't even have understood the feeling of love. It was the perfect innocence of love. He didn't know what he had felt, yet he had just one thought in mind, to have her with him; to feel her presence with him; to do things for her, to have her in his arms, to make her feel special, to do anything that she wants, in other words, what grown people may call, to love her completely.

Well, Surya wasn't given that opportunity. Surya was to leave her, all that he dreamt to do, was denied, by the very person whom Surya wanted to share those moments with. He could've gone back, could've made her fall in love with him but Surya believed that one's love cannot be bought or to be made, it must be earned. It must flow like a river from the heart; no one can 'make' a river, can we? It must come in, naturally. It must flow with all its sounds and dances and cheers and jumps. That's what the magic in seeing that river, in its natural happiness. Surya hence, didn't want to go anymore. He knew he can earn, but her voice, saying him not to come after her, repelled his actions. It's what she said to Surya, which he wanted to obey. He didn't want to make her feel even a little irritation of him, which is much worse, than just not do anything and be alone. But, Krishna couldn't understand this, he wants Surya to have what he needed, he didn't notice the power of Shivani's words, in Surya. He would feel it hard to understand Surya's logic.

Well, Surya couldn't even say that to Krishna. His heart weighed so heavy to even speak. All he did was to gather his wits and say so with whatever energy he had, to Krishna. He's the one that cared. He deserved to know.

"Look Krishna, as a human, as she noticed, the only thing that Shivani had wanted me to do, is to leave her... completely. What lover am I if I don't cherish what she said?"

"Dude this is bullshit! See it from her side; she doesn't even know you... She might've just called it off like every random guy."

"She said she knew me well that day Krishna. She had read the messages right? She did know how much I liked her. She just didn't like me!"

"But Sur..."

"Stop Krishna! What's over is over! Please don't ask me anymore."

"Whatever Surya, but mark this, If there's going to be any girl in the universe who'd match to you, none would ever be as good as Shivani. Know that!"

"Let time answer that."

"I also wanted to tell you something..."

"Yeah?"

"I'm leaving town."

"For holidays?"

"No, I'm going to join in the south. In a residential school and do my schooling for 11th and 12th grade there."

Surya sighed deep. He's now fed up with all the bad things happening around him. His love's gone, His friends who're nearly a family to him had gone and much worse, his best friend Krishna is going too.

"Wow, I don't know what to say Krishna. It's like I'm bankrupt. How is it that everything would go like this? It's a thunder after thunder in a same place! How would anyone bear it?"

"I know Surya; it's just that I have better chances of getting marks there! I won't do anything but study in a residential school, eventually I'll get marks."

"Well, look at me; I said the same things to you when I joined in a residential school. Did you forget?"

"Well, we both are grown now Surya and most of our batch join in those schools too. So, I think anyway it's worth the chance."

"Alright, anyway if it was bad for me, it doesn't have to be bad for you!"

"Hmmm..."

"So, when're you leaving?"

"Tomorrow."

"Great, really, I don't know why God hates me so much!"

"Anyway, at some point we got to separate dude, just think that it's time now! You'd get cool new friends too! A whole new school is a good opportunity for that and I won't be all gone okay? At least once in a month I'll come, at those times I'll see you! Now cheer up! I hate these serious talks of us!"

"Hmm, yea...! Anyway, good luck bro!"

"Hmm... " Krishna went on with the memories he and Surya had cherished before. Surya too, hearing them cheered and continued with some other memories. With all those memories, laughs, fun, talks, Surya and Krishna went on talking through the twilight, till Mr Moon arrived. By the hour of 7:30, both the friends then only noticed that it's now late and got up the benches.

"So Surya, think this is our last frequent talks. Hope there'd be monthly talks from now on."

"Yea, than events, we'll talk about memories here after."

"Which I believe won't be worse."

"Well, memories won't be the same without you anymore Krish..."

"Hey, now don't make me sad! Come on they can be better too! Don't stick with those things. Learn to let go."

"Cool bro! Now I guess this is a good bye then!"

"Yes... Good bye Surya!"

"Good..." Surya cleared his throat. To let out the words from his heart, "Good bye Krishna, enjoy the new school."

"You too Surya... Bye."

Surya and Krishna both went in their own ways. Surya at last saw Krishna for the final time. He won't be there as always as before. It's time to have new elements in Surya's life. All of his environment, his friends, his situations are going to change from now. Who knows what to expect. So, with a little sadness, Surya saw Krishna leave. It was then Surya thought to him,

"Life's moving so fast! Hope it turns out good." And he continued walking to his home.

Chapter 20: Twines of lives, Friendship.

*T*he next day, the sun shone bright. The just ended summer's traces are felt a little, though the morning breeze made everyone fresh. People say, 'Every day is a new day!' Well, this day really looked new. It is a start for the regular routine of Surya's two year voyage. That's the reason why it's so special now. Our boy had stitched his uniforms already. Though Mr Chandrasekhar just informed of the uniforms in the fresher's party, Surya was already aware of it and he made sure that he was ready with it after the school opens.

The uniform was a white with mild red, chequered shirt, with the same mild red plain pant and a canvas white shoe. Surya had been given an ID card, for his class, and was wearing it. His style of wearing it was to place the card in the shirt pocket and twist the cord to make a vine look. He wore the belt which had the emblem of Krya in the buckle. Always, tailor-made suiting does have the reputation.

He looked at himself in the mirror. He did look good. After so many days, he felt good from heart. He did hope to have the best time of his life in Krya. He went up, took his bag and unlocked his Turbo-Drive, and pedalled it to life to get to the bus stand. This time, he's got to go only in the bus. While pedalling, he passed by Krishna's house. Inside, *he saw Krishna and his mum busily packing to leave, while their car and its driver waited for them. He said in his mind, "Good bye buddy, I wish our fates would meet together someday!" Well, bidding bye to him, Surya pedalled faster. He's not supposed to be late. Surya went to the stand, parked his cycle in the parking nearby, and marched fast to the stop, at the other side of the road.*

When he came, he saw Kavya. He didn't like her. He just pretended he never bothered about her and went and sat under the cement roofed bus stop. He never looked at the girls' side. Their presence made Surya really angry. Surya just faced away.

"Why is he behaving like that with us Nisha? He used to be nice right?" Priyanka asked.

"Yea, Even that's what I'm wondering! We were friends from childhood! He'd always speak with us even when he's busy! But what's gotten into him!" Nisha replied.

"Hmmm, well who knows?"

The bus that Surya was made to board the previous day was the one that came to the stop. Surya stood up on seeing it. But the girls reacted in no manner. They didn't board the bus. The bus too, after a moment didn't stop, it just passed by. Surya's anticipation was right. There is the new bus coming too. He too waited.

Later the bus no. 19 came. The new bus was well washed and was shining. Surya gazed at the bus's arrival and saw Kavya. Kavya too noticed Surya staring at her, yet she avoided it. Surya boarded the bus after all the girls boarded it. Surya sat in the second row from the front. The bus was too good especially at the window seat, and Surya travelled happily this time to his school.

The bus curved in slowly and steadily at the roads inside the Krya campus. Surya felt sleepy as the bus journey was about a solid 35 minutes' travel. After getting down the bus, Surya walked the distance to Krya CBSE. The buses usually halt at the Krya's old building, for the State board syllabus students. Surya had to walk from there, through the soccer field, through the school's stage for cultural and assemblies, to Krya CBSE. Surya crossed through them. The view of the Krya CBSE from the soccer field looked like a painting. The C-shaped school's building was artistic with the mild garden that was set up before it. Surya loved the view and was marching towards his class, obviously to meet his only friend till now, Koma.

When entering, Surya saw five guys in the classroom, all of them curious in the benches. There was a tall, fair guy, and two medium complexioned guys whose actions were the main eye-catcher and the other two boys, of medium height, and again one fair, stout boy and one dark average boy was watching the other three. Surya wanted to see what the show was about. The boys never noticed on who was coming; they were so determined at the desk, whose aggressive shouting if were absent, would be considered to them reading cautiously. Surya peeped into what was going on the table. Surya saw those boys, playing a game that Surya too played in the desks of C.B.W., the game *that every school student enjoys, a game a college student remembers, a game that once played would always have a grip on you, a game, that's simply called, 'Pen Fight." Surya was amazed to see a pen-fight game in Krya. It brought back a lot of memories to him. It gave an aroma of C.B.W.'s presence.*

"Wow! A pen-fight! Guys, can I join in next?" Surya asked.

"Well, okay, you can, only in the next game." The medium dark boy replied, with an innocent smile in his face. His smile attracted Surya. It was sweet and innocent, that could make anyone feel good. The boy continued. "Hey, by the way, I'm Dwarakesh."

"Stylish Name!" Surya replied.

"Thanks... and this is Vishnu." Pointing to the tall fair guy, Dwarakesh introduced Vishnu. "This stout here is Ashwin, the one sitting beside me, with the spectacles and a look of a scientist, is Suresh, and the last one there is Mohan."

"Hey guys! I'm Surya."

"So, Surya want to play? The game's over." Suresh asked Surya.

"Of course!! Who said no?" Surya put his bag down and took the pen from his pocket and launched it to the middle region of the three seated table, the basic rule of the pen-fight. Launch the pen, to the desired region, take turns in launching, and attack all the other pens in turns, and the last pen that stays in the table wins. After the launch of Suresh, Dwarakesh, and Vishnu, Surya targeted Vishnu's pen, but

missed it. On each other's turns, Dwarakesh's pen, charged heavily with Surya's and knocked it off the bench, so hard that the pen flew three benches away. Surya was amazed. Clearly, these people are pro's in pen-fights. Yet, Surya wanted to play more. Each and every time he was the first one to go. The three boys were a Ph.D. in pen-fights. They did tricks that nearly made a show out there.

It was nearly 15minutes that Surya was losing. But, he never got tired. This was the 37th match that was going on. This time, Vishnu targeted Surya. After the attack, Surya's pen shot off the table and this time, it landed in a bag.

"Oh! You guys would never change." A girl replied after staring at the guys who shot the pen at her.

"It's alright you give it to us." Dwarakesh said.

The girl bent down and took the pen and gave it to Surya. Surya said thanks and. . .

"Hey I'm Surya." Surya introduced himself.

"I'm Vidya! I've joined in the bio-stream. And this is Nithya and that is Siya."

"Hey!" Siya and Nithya replied.

"Hi!" Surya was amazed on how talkative Vidya is. He just introduced himself with just a 'hi', but she said her name, her stream and introduced two more girls whom for a decency said 'hi' to a just met boy.

"Okay! Next match!" Surya said, but suddenly Mrs Nancy had come in to the class. Everybody stood up to her and wished a good morning. Koma too had come, but Surya didn't notice him then. He shouted. "Koma!"

"Shh..! Silence!" Mrs Nancy said.

"Students, there's been a change in faculties. I'm going to handle the chemistry lab sessions for you from now on, and here, is Mr Ram. He's going to be your class teacher as well as your chemistry teacher." Mrs Nancy said.

The students looked at Mr Ram. He was a unique man. He had a figure that had once played so hard, long hands and legs, though he looked at the age of forty he didn't have a big tummy, a medium sized body, which didn't sync with his head. His head was big in ratio, when compared with the torso. His face features were the main attraction. Though he remained awake, his eyes broadcasted the sandman's sands that could make everyone fall asleep. They always remain half closed.

"Hello children. I'm Mr Ram, as your ma'am said, your chemistry teacher. Though everyone may think Chemistry is a boring subject, I'll make you as interesting as I can. As usual let's have an introduction this class and we'll continue in the second period this afternoon." Mr Ram introduced himself to the class and told this. To tell this, he took a solid 65 seconds, stressing all the vowels as he spoke, without any distinct pronunciation. In a mild voice, that didn't stress his vocal cord.

"Dude, I'm already sleepy!" Koma said to Surya; he noticed Surya, who was focusing the teacher, with all the energy he had to open his eyes. Seeing that, Koma spoke to himself. "He's already slept, with his eyes open!"

After the introduction Mrs Nancy left the class, announcing the children that they had chemistry practical class that day in the last two periods. After she left, Mr Ram as every other teacher, started asking all the names of the student, going to each other's place, and later left the students free during the rest of the hour.

"Dude, come on, let's play" Surya said to Suresh.

"Ok, for me, Dwarakesh can we play?" Suresh asked.

"Yeah, come on." Dwarakesh joined.

Again the four boys started playing the pen-fight. Surya's pen now crash landed to the first bench. He looked that and noted its position. It was near an empty chair in the first row, in the girls' side. But, he can't afford to miss the rest of the game. So he stayed there to look at it. Once that finished, seeing Dwarakesh win, Surya went to take the pen, the chair that was empty when he bent down, to take the pen, was 'mysteriously' occupied by a girl now.

Surya was shocked on seeing that. He knew it was empty at first. By the blink of a second could anyone go occupy it? That too, this girl was new. Surya didn't see her during the first day. He, with a big confusion, looked at her. Seriously, he was shocked on her presence.

How could a girl show up, just like that!? With his eyes wide open, Surya again started the game after looking at her. Surya this time didn't go out of the ring first, but he went out second; As if that was any good. He then asked Vidya,

"Hey, where did that girl come from?"

"Who knows?" Vidya shrugged her shoulders in an action of conveying her unknown.

"Did you notice how she came?"

"Nope."

"I'm playing here, at a second I see an empty chair, then suddenly the next second someone's sitting there!" Surya exclaimed.

Vidya sighed and gave a look, which said "Are you mad?" Surya noticed it and replied,

"Look, I may sound crazy, but that's what really happened!"

"Whatever."

The girl who Surya saw was Jean. She actually joined late in Krya. So, Surya had never seen her before in Krya's premises. Surya noted her being so, still and silent, that looked as if she's sleeping with her eyes open. She did yawn a lot. Her posture noted that she wasn't interested in anything that's happening in the class. Well, to sum up, she looked like Frankenstein's monster, expressionless, breathless, lifeless, and motionless. Surya looked over her for a minute and continued to play the game.

Chapter 21: Forgetting to speak up.

The time was 11:45 on the nose. All the students of the eleventh grade of Krya were indulged in something. Surya was bored after the first period on his pen-fight and was continuously talking with Koma afterwards. Later, bored on that too, the friends started making their own friends. Koma was always the start up. He was the one who first put his nose and introduced himself and later Surya would join in and people who are okay with each other are now a gang.

Well, with this same technique, Koma's old school friend, Vishnu, Ajay, Bala, with Surya and Koma are now a gang. Surya felt that life won't be as bad as he had imagined. He thought life at Krya would become much more interesting than it is now. Surya felt relieved. He felt, that he was causing more trouble to his father. He also thought to make this money worth it. For that he must acquire whatever, happiness, knowledge and experience he shall get in Krya.

So, now having formed a gang, Surya's job was to study and study and study. With this mind-set Surya was eagerly waiting for Mr Xavier's maths class. With just a two minutes delay, Mr Xavier entered the classroom. The tall, skinny, long faced guy came in silently and with his echoing voice, he told the students to sit down at their places. Surya and Koma were sitting in the first bench. The first chapter Mr

Xavier taught though was tough, Surya learned very well the previous day. Surya made him enthusiastic, so that he could not feel the class boring. Surya had his notes ready, pen over the book and was sitting straight.

Well, even the most struggled self-made enthusiasm of Surya, didn't even last for even five minutes with Mr Xavier. What happened was Surya was so energetic that he solved those problems quickly and would tell the answer soon to Mr Xavier. After a few problems like that, when Surya was about to tell the answer for the problem being done now, Mr Xavier signalled to Surya, an expression that would've been scary to toddlers, but was pure irritation for Surya. Mr Xavier, shushed Surya when he was about to tell the answer. His shush was so loud and squeaky that nearly everyone faced Mr Xavier. Then Mr Xavier continued,

"Is there anyone in this class who could tell a boy here that he's not the only one present?"

Surya was so angry on hearing this. We all know Surya. Surya loved his family more. He was soft to everyone. He won't stick on to anything for a long time. He's learned a lot in letting things go. Surya was also a fun guy at first, he loved fun. He had so many beautiful memories with friends, with badminton, with Shivani too, of course that was in his mind alone and also, we saw that when Surya encounters something that he's denied of, he'd accept the fact about it and would try to move on. But, what we didn't see till now was, Surya's anger. Surya's anger is childish. It gets angry a lot all of a sudden and would forget it soon. That's a good habit I guess. People have said anger burns up our mind and actions, it was a pure carrier of bad things etc. well, Surya's anger is not a short-tempered, but he was a short-term tempered.

Well, when Mr Xavier finished telling, Surya got really angry. Though we now know that Surya was short-term tempered, his anger at this time, reached the highest limit it can reach. Surya also, would become angry only if his anger was reasonable. He never liked people disproving him, discouraging him, ordering him. He accepts an advice, but he never accepts an order. To him, any decision that he had ever made was his own choice. The very reason Surya left C.B.W. was that his principal scolded him due to the fact of his bad grades.

Surya was now in a similar situation. He was boiling in the inside that came out with reactions of throwing his pen on the desk. He shrunk his face, and stared angrily at Mr Xavier, who didn't even care to look at Surya. He simply continued with the lesson, whereas Surya stopped listening and just copied the sums that Mr Xavier did on the board. Later as the period got over, Mr Xavier left the class. Everyone stood up except Surya. Surya lost his threshold of respect on Mr Xavier and things once lost in his mind are very hard to get back.

As the period got over, Surya, Koma, Bala, Ajay and Vishnu went to the ground and sat in a lawn. Ajay was the guy, whom we encountered on Surya's first day. He was the one who laughed hysterically and made a whole bench shake. Bala was so silent on the first day that he went unnoticed. Vishnu was also accompanying them.

"*Surya, got a good bulb from Mr Xavier?*" *Ajay teased.*

"*Come on… stop talking about him. He's the only teacher in the world who had hated students answering a question.*"

"*Know your teachers before you know the answers my friend!*" *Ajay said.*

"*Nah, I've seen teachers like him too. They just want themselves to tell the solutions so that they are always smart for the children. I think that's their ego, in knowing something that the children don't.*" *Vishnu said.*

"*Whatever man… I just don't like it.*" *Surya said.*

"*In which stream did you study before Ajay?*" *Koma asked.*

"*CBSE*"

"*Bala?*"

"*CBSE*"

"*How much grades did you both get?*" *Asked Koma, while he was about to take in the spoon to his mouth that carried a load full of curd rice.*

"*10.*" *Both of them replied in chorus. Koma spat out the rice in his mouth and watched the two boys in shock, to which they just smiled.*

"*Toppers!*" *Koma exclaimed.*

"*Hey, CBSE tenth was easy. Most of them scored ten points in the nation.*" *Ajay said.*

"Anyway, let's stop talking about the past… Let's eat! I'm damn hungry." Koma said.

"Surya, I'm leaving, I can't eat anymore. I'm off to class. Bye." Bala said while he got up to leave.

"I'll also come…. wait Bala" said Ajay as he too packed his stuff and was about to leave the place…

"Surya, both of them… 10 pointers…" Koma said.

"Hmmm"

"Think they'll be the Toppers of our class"

"Can't we be Toppers?" Surya asked Koma.

'I don't know Surya… I've never been one.'

'Nobody is born perfect Koma… they improvise themselves.'

'Yes Surya but…'

"Stop… No buts… All that we have to do to become toppers, is to work hard… there're no special ingredient."

"Yes dude… we could be. We will be." Koma exclaimed… he reacted as if Surya had given him a pre battle pep talk.

Both the friends after finishing their lunch went to the class. The next hour was chemistry. Surya always had a dark spot for chemistry. He never could remember those equations, why equations? Surya couldn't even remember the elements in the periodic table. The reason was Surya's mind was analytical. It never liked mugging up the topics. Chemistry too was not that a mugging up subject, but Surya's teachers, from his ninth grade, that is, since chemistry got separated from science in his syllabus, imposed on him to mug up the subject, than making him understand it. For example,

They said,

"When $H_2 + O_2$ combines, we'd get $2H_2O$" but they never told him why or how. Surya found no point in learning something like this. This was the reason he found chemistry boring and unnecessary. Eventually he never spent time in chemistry, which is of course a bad habit for schooling. Well, for the lack of option to leave chemistry, Surya had to chew on this subject till his twelfth grade. With this mentality, the worst thing that happened was, the period fell in the hour just after the lunch break. There's now a lullaby, for the sleep that's sowed.

Surya, half asleep already, was just sitting in his chair next to Koma, who was playing pen fight with Suresh. This was the first class for Mr Ram, as the teacher of chemistry. In not more than five minutes' time, Surya fell asleep, for the boy immediately rested his head on the bench and closed his eyes peacefully. Later, in a few minutes, Mr Ram came to the class. Everybody stood up and wished him a good noon and sat in their places after he nodded. Surya was strongly asleep when all this happened. Koma on noticing him fast asleep called the students who were nearby, to have a look of our sleeping Surya. Then later, after all the laughs were over, he woke up Surya. Surya jolted straight to his chair when Koma woke him up. Surya's first sight was to see Mr

Ram cleaning the board with his duster. He let out a long breath and yawned deeply, wiping his eyes. Koma on seeing him, laughed. Later, Surya asked with a yawn.

"When did he come?"

"Just now." Koma said with a smile.

"How long was I asleep?"

"Who knows? Perhaps, if you could ask me how many know that you were asleep, I can guarantee some answer."

"Huh?"

"Come on, we were enjoying the show of the sleeping beauty, you know? Well, considering the fact that, Surya, you aren't beauty." Koma said.

"Not funny." Surya said, with an expression that had his eyes half closed, brows shrunk to the centre.

"Okay students, stop discussion." Mr Ram said and continued,

"Students, today, we're going to study about solid states. You see, every element, is..." Mr Ram started his class, which was as slow and as sleepy as the lullaby. Surya was already sleepy and the teacher was cultivating that sleep he had.

"Whoa... What's he doing bro??" Surya asked Koma.

"You really think I know?"

"Geez... can this school be any better? Depressing! I always thought my school was the worst of 'em all!" Surya sounded as if he was in vain.

"Calm down alright. Look at the class. Look how fun it is. Look to the left, second row. Look at her notebook. See what she's doing!" Koma said, pointing to a girl. Surya looked at her with a struggle, for opening up his eyes, which were begging to get closed! When he saw her, he noticed that the girl was drawing something.

"Ha-ha! At least she's awake and imaginative." Surya said, laughing.

"Now, look to the last girl in the fourth row!" Surya looked at her, when Koma told. He was much more awake than before now and saw her reading.

"Koma look she's reading!"

"Look closely."

Only then, Surya saw that the girl was reading a book called, 'the chicken soup.' he was surprised on seeing that.

"Bro, that book is much bigger, to learn to make a chicken soup!"

"Finally look at our Nandhu." Surya looked back at Nandhu. Nandhu was completely closing his eyes, but he also was nodding to the lesson. Surya and Koma were laughing so hard on seeing Nandhu's actions, which produced funny noises to the whole class. Most of the boys and girls looked at these boys' laughs and they too laughed. Nearly the whole class went giggling on seeing Nandhu and the class became restless, producing funny sounds. For all this, Mr Ram, who was *facing the board while he was teaching, just said, "Stop Discussion." again.*

"Stop discussion!" Koma imitated his dialogue silently to Surya who again started laughing as before. Mr Ram never even looked at what was happening in the class. He continued on and on with the same class in the same tone, that if recorded and showed to him, he'd have his snoring coming up in less than two minutes.

"Dude, he's turning, stop laughing." Koma said to Surya. Surya controlled his laughter. Mr Ram turned and continued his teaching. Once he started, Surya saw him teach. Surya looked at him closely. Mr Ram was looking at the ceiling of the class when he was teaching. His chin inclined at a perfect 60°. Than seeing the students, he was seeing the whole white ceiling. Surya saw this and was laughing within him.

"Who's sitting there?" Koma said, looking at the top and when Koma looked at where Mr Ram was seeing, Surya was out of control. He just stood up and asked Mr Ram for permission to go to the restroom and went out at once. Later, as Surya went by, the whole class heard a big laughter echoing through the corridors. For when Koma alone knew that it was Surya and for what reason he had laughed so. Surya later entered the class. Both Surya and Koma smiled at each other for what had happened, and was enjoying the whole chemistry class the same way.

After the chemistry class, the students were told that it was their Computer science or biology period that hour. Surya and Koma were of Computer Science stream. The students of the computer stream were to move to the computer lab, during the hour. They were packing all their stuff, to go there, when Vidya came.

"You could've laughed here itself Surya, Why going out? We all heard for what you did, called laugh."

"Ha-ha... I'm sorry, I just couldn't control my laugh, you see look at that guy! Damn... the craziest guy I've ever seen in the history of teachers!"

"Maybe, So, Surya, are you on Facebook?"

"Of course, who isn't?" Surya said.

"Tell me, what's your Facebook ID?"

"Ho..." Surya suddenly stopped telling.

"Hmmm?"

"Don't laugh okay."

"Ahem." Vidya cleared her throat and nodded.

"Hotshot Surya." Surya said, with a shy.

"Hotshot?"

"Yea"

"I could keep that in mind."

"Okay, got to go bye Vidya, come Koma!"

Surya and Koma went to the computer lab. The first thing Surya caught seeing in it, is the lab's air conditioners put on. The same effect from the A.K.R.S., Surya gulped in, yet this time he knew he'll enjoy it. Surya saw his classmates coming in. Except Vishnu and Ajay, Surya, Bala, Koma were in the lab. They were to sit down on the floor during the theory hours in the lab and later, when they are to be in the practical session, they'd be allotted their respective computers to work upon. Being the theory session now, Surya and Koma like all the other students now present in the lab, sat down on the floor, with Surya, anticipating how his computer teacher will be like. He's seen Mr Ram, so funny now, not making much of a talented impression, a chemistry lab ma'am Mrs Nancy, straight-forward and the likable type, also the Physics teacher Mr Sundar, Nothing that special with him, his English ma'am, Ms Shobha, the classic teacher, and not to forget our very own, Mr Xavier, the unexplainable. He had a good two long days in Krya. Well, this is the first time he's going to meet his computer science ma'am. Surya was waiting for the ma'am to arrive.

"What was her name?" Surya asked.

"Preethi" Koma replied.

"Hmm, let's see. We're having a very big range of teachers. Let's hope she's good."

While the boys were speaking Mrs Preethi arrived. She was in her mid-30s. She came in and everyone stood up and wished her. The first few minutes of the period went on as every other subject's first classes were. Then, after for nearly ten minutes, Jean entered. She came in and sat at the end of the girls' row.

"Who the hell is that girl?" Surya asked.

"Why're you asking?"

"No, this morning she came mysteriously at the class while I was playing the game, I've never seen her before too. Even Vidya doesn't know who that is. That's why."

"Well, wait, ma'am will ask her that." Koma said. As he said, Mrs Preethi too asked Jean.

"And you are?" Mrs Preethi asked.

"My name's Jean ma'am, I'm from the U.A.E." Jean replied. Surya and Koma looked at each other with awe.

"Where're you staying dear?"

"I'm staying at my uncle's house ma'am."

"Okay, so class, being your first day, there won't be any lessons taken today, is the phrase that you are expecting. Well, I suppose this is your second day at Krya. Hope you people got enough time talking. Let's go on with the class." Mrs Preethi said and continued teaching with the power-point presentations she had. She was teaching with them to conserve the time of writing the topics down. She was the best teacher Surya ever had. She was fun, not 'unnecessarily' strict and was crystal clear at what she says. Surya listened well the whole class.

Koma chanted the whole class, showing his 'performance'. Surya saw Jean. She looked different from other girls. He wanted to be a friend with Jean. She somehow was familiar to him in his heart. Well, who knows what made him feel so? So he at times saw her and listened to the class.

Later, after the computer class, Surya had the Chemistry lab session. It was a two periods' session. Poor Surya, Krya had nine periods a day which was really tiring him. So, from the computer lab located at the first floor, Surya went to the chemistry lab at the ground floor. There he met Mr Durai, the lab attendant who was always called as 'Durai sir' by the students of Krya. The old students of Krya, on entering the lab, started speaking with him as if he was a friend and not a faculty.

"Hi boys, how's eleventh standard?" Durai sir asked.

"Fun sir, but not much signs for friendship till now." Nandhu replied.

"Hmmm, what's scarce for that? You'll all end up good." Durai sir said. Later when he saw Surya, he called out...

"And who's this Amul baby?" He said, laughing. 'Amul baby' is a term that is commonly used in India to note a person who is chubby and cute. Surya on noticing that it was him, who was referred, smiled wanly. He never liked such comments. He knew he was fat, yet the few days of having the medium sized body, made him feel good. Then later, after the badminton match, after Shivani leaving him, after all the hardships that followed since then, Surya never really cared about playing, that resulted in him becoming obese again. Which

when at times like this, he dislikes it. Anyway, overcoming that too, Surya smiled.

"Hi sir, my name's Surya."

"Nice name! Surya, you're looking so cute! See how chubby and how cute he is Nandhu!" *Durai sir said.*

"He he... Yea, Damn I can't get these looks." *Nandhu said. Nandhu meant his words, because the poor boy only weighed 43kgs in his eleventh grade, looking as lean as a pencil.*

"You have to be eating for that Nandhu; you must stop playing soccer too, if you want a body like this." *Durai sir told.*

"If that's the case I don't want to be good-looking sir!" *Nandhu said, laughing in between his body vibrations. Surya was simply looking at these two people blank. Later, with all the casual talks, Surya and Koma went inside the lab.*

"Good evening students!" *Mrs Nancy said, while she was entering the lab, she continued,*

"Look students, I was told that you people are going to study only the portions of twelfth standard topics for your chemistry lab classes, which eases up all our works. I have to teach only few topics for a whole of two years and you people have more time to read on the portions and thorough it. So, the exercises you'll be studying are these." *Saying this, Mrs Nancy handed over a few sheets to the students.*

Surya went over the sheet he got. The first page read 'Salt analysis.'

"SALT ANALYSIS!" Koma screamed.

"Yes, what do you think?" Nandhu said.

"Oh crap!"

"Why? What's happening? Why're you screaming?" Surya asked puzzled. He never knew what it was.

"Dude! Don't you know what Salt Analysis is?" Koma asked in a desperate voice.

"Yea, I'm having it right here!"

"If you're going to make dumb dialogues I'll punch your face!"

"Come on tell me!" Surya asked.

"What do you think you will do with these texts in your hand?" Koma asked, pointing to the sheet of paper that looked like tables which looked like matching references.

"Well, from these tabular look, I suppose it's a referencing material for the experiment we're going to do. You know, like logarithm tables." Surya replied with a shrug, in a way meaning that it was an easy task.

"Well, for your info, what you said was correct, with just a slight change. You won't refer the paper, but you'll have to memorize the whole sheet. With all the observations for the tests and their results, including the different tests for acid and basic radicals for the salt you're about to get." Koma said. Surya's jaw dropped. He stared at Koma in shock.

"What!!!!" Surya exclaimed.

"Yep, you heard him!" Nandhu said.

"Oh my God! How am I supposed to do this?" Surya said in a desperate tone.

"That's why the two years' time dude." Nandhu said.

"With a sheet like this, I'll need extra time dude!" Surya said, just then, Mrs Nancy started her instructions to the students,

"Look guys, all you have to do is, have a read through the papers, look at them, and do the experiments first and note down your observations in your note. Only this day you'll be having your paper with you, from next class, you have to do it on your own. Which means, you people must memorize it now itself. Now off you go, and do your experiments."

"Yea, Yea whatever." Koma said.

The people in the lab were doing their experiments busily. They were playing with them. Surya saw those guys the way he saw Krishna, Preethi, Divya and Neha when they were playing shuttle. Predicting what's going to happen they were doing those experiments. Well, Surya didn't even observe which salt he got. Surya felt some strange feeling in his stomach. The work everyone did made him tired, exhausted, irritated.

"I hate this." Surya said to Koma who was standing in the table before him, facing the guy next to Surya.

"Me too." Koma said smiling.

"Do you know what to do?"

"No."

"Me neither."

"Let's ask someone." Koma said this and searched for anyone who would really care to at least help. Surya saw Vidya nearby.

"Hey Vidya, what should I do?"

"Later... I'm busy."

"Yeah okay tell."

"Huh? I told you! I'm busy!"

"Come on, this is my first lab in my life. Help me out will you?"

"Haven't you studied in tenth?"

"We had, but my dude did everything for me that time."

"You're expecting me to do this for you eh? In your dreams Surya."

"No, I'm not telling you to do this for me Tell me what to do! Please!"

"Ok, first take the salt in your hand, and see what its colour and appearance are. Look, this one's white and powdery, note it down. Then, look for the tests one by one, do what's told in them- in the description of them, whatever you get, write it down, then finally, there are columns for your Acid radical and Base radical, do them and

your experiment is finished okay?" Vidya sighed after telling this, for the girl told all of this in a single breath. Poor girl is always a fast talker.

"Okay, what are acid radical and base radical?" Surya asked. The moment he asked it, the whole lot of people nearby him looked in shock. He turned around to look why the class was suddenly silent and noticed that everyone was looking at him awkwardly. Surya too felt the same awkwardness. He gulped and asked Vidya,

"Why is everyone staring at me?"

"...Because, as an eleventh grader, you just asked the dumbest question of all."

"Why?"

"Don't you know what a salt is?"

"The white powder we put in food?"

"UGH!!!" Vidya said, in anger, because, this was too dumb than the previous question.

"Look Surya... Stop humiliating yourself dude... Seriously don't you know that a salt is a mixture of an acid and a base?"

"It is?" Surya looked around, that's the time he realised nearly all of his dumbness in asking those two questions... He cleared his throat, looked away, and coughed a little; he didn't know what else to say or to do... The crowd was seeing him, giving a look of laughter, He, *standing in the middle of it, to which he'd have laughed if someone else had been there as him. Why someone else, he laughed at his own foolishness and said,*

"Oops, my bad... Okay guys, continue..." Surya said smiling. Everyone in the lab looked at Surya equal to a slug, irritated on its presence. Surya noticed the way everyone behaved later. Just because he asked such a bad question, thereafter, he was branded as a dumb boy. He didn't want to ask anything about salts again. Whenever he heard the word 'salt', what came into his mind was the humiliation he got. Surya didn't like it. Thereafter, he came to a conclusion in himself, to not to ask questions in class. He feared of being humiliated again. Funny, the single look from students gave the boy a whole impression on himself, and making up a decision, that straight away drives him to become unsuccessful. Surya didn't know that. So, the first strike on the second day of Krya happened... It's forgetting to speak up.

Chapter 22: Forgetting Self-Confidence.

*S*urya went home that day. He was so embarrassed after the events in the lab. He and Koma walked silently down the road to the buses and boarded them. Then, Surya found buses nineteen and twenty combined, making a single bus for the route of both. Surya and Nandhu now sat together. They spoke and Nandhu slept. Later, when Surya had come to his stop, he got down at first, later the ex-C.B.W. girls got down. He never liked them for except Priyanka and Nisha. Surya never looked at them, for if he did, he'd have to see the others too... especially Kavya.

Not caring for them, Surya went to his home. This was a long day in Krya for Surya. So, the first thing he did was turning the TV on and throwing the bag in the corner and fall on to the sofa. Surya was watching one of his favourite shows, Ben 10. Who wants to grow up? While he was watching, it was then he was reminded of Vidya asking Surya about the Facebook ID. So, Surya switched on his PC and started surfing for the Facebook.

Surya once logged, saw a friend request from Vidya. He thought 'So Fast! Girl I just got home!' Surya accepted her friend request and started to search on her friends. He found Nithya, Siya and nearly a few more girls of Krya. Later, he went down more to see Suresh's account. He gave a request to him and later on, to nearly each and every members of Krya. Only then he realised he missed Koma. So, searching for his name, Surya immediately saw his account pop in front of him and was laughing on seeing him in his red striped glittery shirt, with his teeth-spilling smile. He gave him a request too. Surya then thought: what if he could find Jean's account. Maybe he could get along with her.

Surya then, typed her name, and searched, bad luck for him he never found her account. Later, after a few minutes, he got a lot of notifications telling the people that he sent requests had accepted it. He then, after a few more minutes, browsed on in the 'People you may know' section, There! He found Jean's account. There, he saw her smiling from her left ear to the right, while standing in a bus.

"Whoa! She can smile!" Surya said, laughing.

Then, without any delay, he gave her a friend request. Later, Koma popped up in a message box, and Surya and Koma were talking till 7 p.m. Surya then, tired of talking with him, bid him bye and was about to log out. Then he moved his mouse to the 'log out' button. But he thought of looking something else. He clicked the search bar, looked over to his keyboard and started typing Shivani's name. It's a dead man's wish for him to see her pic. After a while, he saw her account's name, listing just after he typed 'S' He saw, 'Hotshot Surya' and 'Shivani Shiv' one after the other. Surya smiled for a moment, he admired at the beauty of his name and Shivani's being together. Surya then clicked on to it and then saw the whole gang of Shivani, in the cover pic. Surya kept his hand all over the pic, covering each and every one else's faces and looked at Shivani. He then let out a long breath, telling to himself, 'Why, even after all these things I've faced with you, still some voice is telling that you're mine, and all that I have to do is wait?' Well, who knows? Love's talent is in its mysterious forces and its mystic voices right? Later, Surya went to his home page and eventually to the log off button. Then a final notification popped. Surya opened it and it read 'Jean Jan' accepted your friend request.

"Oh-ho-ho! There's a twist!" Surya said.

Later, Surya refreshed his chat options. Yet he saw Jean offline. So, he just went to see his new friend's pictures on Facebook. There he saw nearly thousands of pictures of Jean. He now realised that she wasn't as spooky as he thought. Later, on scrolling through the pics, he saw someone calling her 'Tingu'.

"Huh? What's this Tingu?!" Surya thought to himself. Later, on seeing that word in a number of comments and statuses, only then Surya realised that it was her nick name. He felt it funny. He also realized that she was never this type and was also as open-mouthed as him. Surya after nearly an hour or so logged out of it and went. He was feeling good for having a good day at school. Though he got a little embarrassed in the end, he had a good memory to cheer up with. He also had the bad memory of Mr Xavier, in his maths class; he later decided to ignore that man. He was now not worthy in Surya's mind.

Later, Surya took out the chemistry sheet Mrs Nancy had given him. He tried to memorize it. He just didn't know how or to his unconscious mind, it didn't understand why and it didn't want it to be remembered too. Surya tried and tried till midnight, yet, he couldn't get off the first page of the sheet. Later, fed-up on the sheet, he threw it away and kept it aside.

Surya then decided to sleep. He closed his eyes. When he did, his mind visualised the embarrassment he had got in the lab. He jolted up the bed. His inner voice scolded him.

"Great… You couldn't even remember the simple text from the three paged stuff, yet, you desire for a good night sleep eh?" It said.

His inner voice just started the engine with those words, later on, all the stuff started running in Surya's thoughts. He now started thinking; he spoke to himself through the mirror.

"Huh, three pages! Can't I just read three pages? I can do it! Why can't I?" Surya said and he got off the bed and started reading the paper that had the salt analysis. Time went on… the clock ticked at 1, 2 and went on, whereas Surya was still continuing with the first page, struggling to fuel it in the mind, Surya looked in the mirror. Something felt bad. He looked trapped. The paper he had in his hand looked as if he had himself cuffed. He then again went into the pool of thoughts.

"What if I can't? What if I fail? It's been two hours now, yet, I'm here juggling with the first page. Oh my God, if I can't pass on with just

this… *How will I ever jump to the theories, not only this subject, I still have Physics, Computer Science… OH! I really forgot Maths! How will I ever complete all those if I struggle with just this damn Salt Analysis till this late hour!" thinking of this, a stark terror struck Surya's heart. He got the strike to his first blow. His courage to take on the subject fell. Surya's mind filled up with a fright that saw no solution. His mind was flooded with a thought of no escape. His thoughts were jumping straight to the place of him being a failure. It caused the fire of fright to demolish and burn all of Surya's confidence. It gave him a fear of losing; it made him think that failure is bad, where he didn't have the strength to regain himself and get over the fright and think out his problems. He feared of facing his failures, without even having any. He was thinking of running away from his problems, when he didn't have anything chasing him. He was being afraid of nothing but a strong illusion.*

What he had was a fear, which experienced people take it lightly, strong willed people take it easily and people who tasted success never even care about it. But, let's look at Surya and his life in a short recap. It was Surya's very own decision to join in A.K.R.S. His decision grounded him deep down. Later, it was his heart's decision to make him love Shivani, which we all know how it ended. Later, though his mind and heart combined in a decision for his badminton, fate had decided a grave failure, that made his hard work and happiness go away. Thinking of ourselves in Surya's situation right now, we can possibly guess what he would've thought. Well, with that, what he thought was,

"All my decisions went in vain, nobody likes me truly, and nothing went right to me so far. How should I expect this to come out well?" Surya thought to himself. He couldn't find an answer to his question. His heart was flooded with fear and pain. For an event that may or may not happen in 2 years, he was scared now. What do we say for this behaviour, foolishness or over-cautious? Well, it's foolishness out of over-cautiousness.

He didn't have any self confidence in him. He didn't have one good success to tell about him, he didn't have any living soul that could encourage him either. So, what would a teenager do now? A teenage mind, in its very own beauty, imagines a way lot of things that saw no end. So, with all this, over-cautious foolishness, Surya bid bye to the confidence he had in him that night.

"Okay I'm thinking too much. Let me sleep this out." Surya said and went to bed.

Chapter 23: New Knots.

"*L*ook students, this is the first law of Newton's. It states, 'An object at rest stays at rest and an object in motion stays in motion with the same speed and in the same direction unless acted upon by an external force.' Now..." Mr Sundar said, teaching the chapter, 'Laws of Motion.'

It's been a week in Krya. The classes went on the same way as it was. Yet, there were few changes that happened through this week. Surya became more attentive to the Chemistry class, which was not much effective. He tried to listen in Mr Xavier's class, yet each and every syllable from his mouth made Surya hate him, Surya's computer science and English classes were the only interesting classes to him because only in them, Surya found a comfortable platform to speak up, to at least have a conversation with the teacher. Surya had always told Koma that it will be really good if all of his classes be like English and Computer Science. Well, we've never discussed any of our Physics classes haven't we, both theory and Practical? Well, let's not wait for them, because in this auspicious day, Surya had a small shift of periods, which shows each and every details of his yet favourite physics subject. Let's go to class shall we?

"Student's, let's consider a tyre rolling in the ground on its own. What do you think will happen in two minutes?"

"The tyre will lose its speed and it will stop sir!" Surya said.

"Good. So, why does the tyre lose its speed? Nobody disturbs the tyre, yet why does it fall off with the speed decreasing?" Mr Sundar asked.

"Sir, there is a disturbance in the tyre sir." Ajay said.

Everyone looked at him. Later, Mr Sundar asked him, "And, that is?"

Surya deeply wanted to tell the answer, yet, the only thing that stopped him telling was that, he didn't know it.

"Friction of course! And due to this, the tyre slows down, still validating Newton's law." Ajay said.

"Absolutely! What's your name?" Mr Sundar asked. There, only there, Surya became startled once more. Surya's main achievement was to get hold of the teacher, to make him know his name; which is like a ticket saved for a movie. When a teacher knows a boy's name, it is obvious that the student had impressed the teacher and signifying an idea of that student being an above average one in the class. Well, now, though Surya had told an answer, it wasn't that enough for getting the name, whereas, the job Surya had, was now finished sooner and smarter by Ajay.

"Ajay Sir!"

"Good Ajay, Now, let's look at the second law..."

"There goes the topper's fame!" Koma said.

"*Will you shut up? I told you a million times, not to call him a topper!*" Surya whispered, shouting at Koma.

"*Surya, don't be foolish. Look, if you want to be emotional that's fine, but you're being insanely stupid by being like this. Not cool bro. Not... cool.*"

"*Buzz off!*"

Surya was getting hold of his anger a lot in the days of Krya. He barely made some friends. The so-called gang was dissolved only two days ago. Bala and Ajay were a lot closer and Vishnu found some new friends, and moreover, it's only Koma and Surya again. Koma yet, goes and joins with some of the boys at Krya, in the very same class. All they do with him is tease him and have a good time. Surya didn't know whether Koma knows it or not, but Surya didn't like Koma allowing the other guys to tease him. So, when Koma went on with these guys, Surya retreated and never got on with those guys.

Krya had a vast opposite environment to what Surya had experienced before in C.B.W. C.B.W. was not a school for the rich. It was a school that offered good education with cheaper fees. It was funded by I.E.C., and the students who studied were from middle class families. Surya grew in that environment. A place where friendships are the far most important things and nobody in the school spent much more than ten rupees for the samosas in the lunch break. Whereas in Krya, if you snatch an eighth grader's purse, you might have the luck to at least find three hundred bucks in it. The richness in the environment, the rich attitude of the students and their behaviour, made Surya feel small.

Surya saw people spending money so generously, which was worth for hundreds of rupees, each and every day. The environment of rich people was signified with the flow of money and the flow of language. The talks those people spoke, from 'what the hell' to the three-starred words, everything signified the whole western civilization, and no Indian traces. They never cared for India, they always awed upon the other countries. The mentality of Krya's students had to be noted. These people will call you 'Nerd' if you score high, 'dumb' if you score low, 'show-off' if you perform, 'alien' if you don't and if you're out of a herd and all alone, not following their culture, they're always ready to ground you at home.

OH! We're off the story right? Now, this environment sowed Surya irritation. He was better off at home, than here. Whenever he gets an answer that he doesn't wants, he gets angry and stops talking. Surya similarly stopped talking even now. He just listened to Mr Sundar's class, telling to himself, to make Sundar ask his name next. Then, Mr Sundar's class got over. It was physics practical classes for the next one hour. Surya had to go to the lab, while Koma was busy going for the rest-room for the fifteenth time. Surya fed up on waiting for him each and every period while he goes to the rest-room, started off to the lab. He was climbing up the stairs, for the lab being in the first floor. Surya while walking up, he noted that Jean too was walking alone.

He thought it was good to speak to her now and yet, was thinking on how to start the conversation. Suddenly, 'Tingu' came to his mind.

"Hi Tingu!" Surya said.

Jean turned and saw him with wide opened eyes on who was calling her, and she saw Surya smiling stupidly.

"How did you know?" She asked after a wan smile.

"Facebook." Surya said.

"Well, don't tell that to anyone or I'll kill you." Jean said.

"Ha-ha, yea okay, I'm Surya by the way."

"Okay."

"Who kept that name, Tingu?"

"My sister."

"Oh, okay, bye!" Surya said. That conversation was awkward enough for the day. Surya was out of topics for now and then he was thinking on continuing with Jean in Facebook later.

Surya then rushed to the lab. He was waiting eagerly to see his teacher. Last week went on with chemistry practical session, to which he had just missed the lab till now. Later, after a few minutes, Ms Anne came. She looked young. She was the youngest faculty of Krya. Surya was now feeling good. It's better to have a teacher who's on the same generation right? So, feeling good he just listened to what she said.

"Hey guys, I'm Anne. I'll be handling the physics lab session for you all these two years."

"I thought this period was the games hour, and she's our games teacher" Koma said.

"Not funny." Surya said, teasing.

"Even for this you'll laugh bro." Koma said in his squeaking voice, and then both the friends shared a laugh.

"Dude, she's looking so calm and soft. She barely speaks right?" Koma asked.

"Yeah, I don't know how people stay this way!" Surya replied.

"Let's check it out." Saying this Koma stood up and called ma'am. And when she came near him, Surya watched on to Koma to what he was about to do.

"Ma'am what's your age ma'am?" Koma asked.

"Huh?" Ms Anne asked.

"Your age ma'am!"

"Why do you want to know?"

"Just general knowledge ma'am."

"Well, you first study what's given to you; later on if you get time, know about all general knowledge." Ms Anne said with a smile.

"Ma'am c'mon tell ma'am." Surya joined on.

"What's with you two!?"

"Ma'am he's telling that you're about twenty seven and I'm telling that you'd be not more than twenty four. We both are betting on whose right. That's why we're asking ma'am." Surya said.

"Now, don't you guys have anything else to speak?"

"No ma'am please tell ma'am." Koma said

"Alright, I'm 25, that makes both of you lose the bet. So, thinking about that, me being the winner, what's the prize? Tell me."

"Hahahahaaaahahhahaa!!!" both the boys started laughing.

"Why're you laughing?"

"Ma'am it's you who's lost!" Surya said.

"Why?"

"Ma'am I saw your Facebook account yesterday. And it clearly stated that you were born in January 13, 1988, making you 25 years old only by this Jan of 2012. So, the one who's wrong is you." Koma told.

"Anyway, both of you were wrong right?"

"No ma'am, our bet was to know whether you told the truth or the lie. I bet that you would tell a lie, and he bet the otherwise and you made me win!" Surya said.

"Being the first day, I'm not going to do anything to you guys. Now stop laughing and do something productive." Ms Anne said and went.

"Dude, I think she's the friendliest teacher that's ever going to be in this Godforsaken school." Surya said.

"Yea bro. Good pull by the way." Koma said.

"What?"

"The twist of telling ma'am about the bet, that it's about her answer being a lie or truth."

"Come on, even I saw the movie."

"You did?"

"Yes, don't tell me that this idea was yours. I too saw this scene in a movie. That's why I too spoke the same dialogues."

"Ha-ha!!! Bro, even if I search the whole school, I won't be getting a friend like you!" Koma said, tapping at Surya.

Later, that evening Koma and Surya were walking towards the buses. Surya saw Priyanka and her gang coming behind him. So, walking at a faster pace, they reached Koma's bus. He went inside to keep his back and come out. Surya while waiting for him to come saw Priyanka pass him. She too on seeing him came by.

"Hey Surya, Remember me?" Priyanka asked.

"What's this Priyanka? Why're you asking like that? How could I ever forget you?" Surya said.

"Oh, guess what? I saw a boy named Surya who doesn't even tell a 'hi' or 'bye' to me, he didn't even tell me that he's going to study in my school, not even looking at me while I'm passing, not wanting to speak too. Think he's become a big celebrity that he forgot a common girl like me or I think he's got so busy with his new friends that he forgot about me."

"You're killing me." Surya said.

"Then what? Why aren't you speaking with me and Nisha nowadays?"

"I don't see anyone nowadays!"

"Yea right! I'm in England and you're in U.S. I forgot that."

"Come on Priyanka! Enough!" Surya said. Priyanka's bombardment made him speechless. He couldn't say that it's because of Kavya that he's avoiding her and also that he didn't want to hear the 'Priyanka' chanting whenever he crosses. So he tried to make up stories.

"Look Priyanka, it's not that I forgot you and all. Just, you're with your own gang, and I don't know anybody else from it. It'd be awkward if I just come and speak with just you in the herd. That's why..."

"You're lying..." Priyanka said abruptly.

"What?" Surya asked, smiling with a frown in his face.

"I've known you since fifth grade Surya. I know your face when you lie. Now tell the truth!" Priyanka ordered, only when she spoke, Kavya called Priyanka.

"Priyanka!" she shouted, then on seeing both Surya and Priyanka talking, she gave out a naughty smile and wobbled her head, telling...

"Oh... Sorry for the interruption, *ahem* you carry on Priyanka carry on!" She said and giggled and went inside the bus.

Surya couldn't hold on to his temper anymore. He just asked bluntly.

"Were you in love with me?"

"What? Why are you asking that?" Priyanka asked, puzzled.

"It's because of all this I stopped talking with you! Whenever I pass by, this crack head always calls out your name and is killing me."

"Hey, you're taking it seriously? Come on, she's jobless Surya! Always she does it like this. Don't take these things seriously."

"I don't know! We're friends from childhood. Yet she's always doing this and it irritates me. If she continues this I'd probably slap her."

"Oh calm down Surya, I'll tell her to stop, don't be angry. Cool down okay! And do you have a mobile with you?"

"What question is this huh? How wouldn't I have?" Surya said, smiling.

"Okay, give your number, and I'll text you!"

"Here it is…" Surya gave his no. and Priyanka noted it in her hand and soon she went to board her bus.

Surya turned back. He saw Koma staring at him with his eyes open and his big mouth giving a naughty smile with his first two teeth peeping out. Surya saw that and laughed at him.

"So, what's happening here?" Koma asked in a tone of tease.

"India vs. Pakistan cricket match."

"Oh! Who won?"

"India."

"Oh! It seemed like a draw to me."

"What're you saying?"

"Dude! Can't you see? She likes you bro!"

"Stop it you stupid dog! She and I are friends from childhood so…"

"So? There's no reason that there can't be any love!"

"Look, you heard her right? She told there are no such things like that for her in me. She told remember?"

"No."

"Why? What did your donkey ears doing that time?"

"Oh, perhaps you didn't hear. She never said she's not in love with you Surya!"

"Well, if that is so, she never said she's in love with me did she?"

"Well, she never denied it when you asked."

"Look bro, she's far too good to look at a guy like me. I told you about Shivani right? I'm worth only that much dude, no girl would love me."

"Why? Is it because you're fat?"

"Yes. Obviously."

"Well, you know what, I'd pay a billion bucks, if I had any, to become like you. The physical appearance never concerns a girl. If that is so, nearly 75% of Indian men would die unmarried."

"Look, anyway, she's my friend I can't think like that about her."

"Dude, she's just your friend. Not your sister."

"If you speak like that..." Surya launched at Koma to slap him playfully, but soon he heard the screeching whistle of the games teacher and he went to his bus. On boarding the bus, he saw his favourite second row already been seated and he sat in the fifth row of the bus. Next to his row, it was Priyanka who was sitting. Surya looked at her and smiled slightly and sat. He was happy that Kavya didn't tease him now and all were sorted out. He never believed in what Koma told and Surya was just looking at the window, with the sun descending on to the ground gently.

Chapter 24: Mystery of Priyanka...

"*H*ey!" Surya said. He was just coming from the bus that had been stopped in the school campus. While he came, he just saw Jean walking in front of him. Only yesterday he and Jean were speaking on Facebook about Jean's old school in the Emirates. Surya and she had a fun time in school with Koma. They were becoming good friends as they had a thing common. Neither of them liked Krya. Their speeches would mostly be on the topic on how bad Krya is.

It's actually a long time from the second week of Krya for Surya. This is the wet September month for the people in Krya. They had shoved up an umbrella in their backpacks with their water bottles. Droplets that fell to the ground sounded like the bells in the environment. The cold breeze shivered and soothed the people who were walking in the path between the overgrown shrubs, which caressed the body with their wet leaves, like a kiss from nature. The morning breeze went through the hairs, like the path of a river in the dense forest, chilling the skin that has missed touch of nature with the black forest of hairs, which made anyone fresh and drowsy at the same time; making us inhale fresh humid air deep and stand still for the whole moment, to enjoy our nature's gift, to enjoy our presence in one of its own pure, young and innocent beauty. This beauty was accompanied by the birds, which also enjoyed nature in their own way; chirping and wobbling *their whole body, pulling off the water from their feathers. The smell of the land, tied up all the senses to the heart, ultimately making the full inner soul, stay at peace with the still painting of the nature.*

In this pleasant presence, Surya and Jean were walking in this same beautiful place, sharing an even more beautiful friendship that too, was so young and innocent.

"Hey Surya...! Another day in heavenly hell!" Jean said.

"Ha-ha... So true J" Surya laughed. He found the name Jean very funny to say, so he shorted it out to just J.

"So, what do you think will be our dangers today?"

"Let's see, the first period is English, not much of a danger I think."

"For you... for me, this one's also a bloody damn danger. Shobha is crooked to me Surya. She leaves of all the boys and is killing us girls."

"Yes, but I don't understand one thing." Surya said.

"What?"

"If she's killing all girls, why is she killing you too?" Surya said with a naughty laugh.

"I'll kill you, idiot."

"Okay calm down! Later it's chemistry, not a danger nor a rescued mission, pure dumbness that is."

"Obviously, Then it's physics."

"*Fun for me!*"

"*Boring for me.*"

"*Ow, why are you so zombie-ic?*" Surya said.

"*Ow, why are you so childish?*" Jean countered.

"*Ok! Then, ahhh! It's games hour next to physics today!*"

"*Finally…! Peace!*"

"*Then it's computer science!*"

"*Oh my God…! After lunch it's TWO HOURS OF MATHS!!!!!!!*" Jean exaggerated.

Both of them stared at each other. All those energy that nature gave, was dropped on so low. Surya and Jean nodded their heads in disappointment. Later, finally Surya continued,

"*And finally chemistry lab.*"

"*Did you finish the two salt analyses?*"

"*Yes, copying is easy… writing it on our own is the difficult thing.*"

"*Good, give me your note when we get to class. I'll start writing it.*"

"*Okay. Hey, there's Koma. Now see how I set him off.*"

"*Hey guys! Nice to see you! Cool weather right?*" Koma came in with wide hands, to Surya.

"*Did you finish the salt analysis work?*" Surya asked seriously.

"*HUH!??? WHAT WORK!!!!*" Koma shouted. Surya knew Koma would never have completed it, or to be precise, he knew that Koma never knows about it.

"*Dude, analysed observations of seven salts, everybody submitted to ma'am yesterday itself! You're asking now!?*" Jean joined to tease Koma.

"*Jean! You serious!?*"

"*Yup!*"

"*Well how about you two? Have you completed?*"

"*Yes bro, we two sat after 3:40 and completed it, and submitted yesterday itself! We later went on in the five o'clock bus trip. You only rushed yesterday remember?*" Surya added.

"*What do I do? What do I do?*" Koma shouted and started running to the class to ask if someone had their notes yet. When he ran, Jean and Surya did a high five and started walking to the class. When they went, they saw Koma staring at them angrily at the entrance itself. By this time, he'd have got teased on by the students for asking lamely about a submission of a work that has never been given.

"*Why you two!*" Koma said and charged upon both Jean and Surya.

"*He only started it!*" Jean said to Koma.

"Dude, wait, wait, WAIT!!!" Surya said to angry Koma, while he started to chase him.

Surya threw his bag to Jean and started running furiously towards the corridor, while Koma chased him.

Koma and Surya later stopped on seeing Ms Shobha coming to the class and both these friends were walking slowly, yet punching each other's stomach with their heads down to the ground.

Days always passed this much pleasantly in Krya. Surya worked hard in school, well to be precise, only in computer science, physics and English, in which, the only subject that requires hard work was physics. He started hating Mr Xavier and eventually the subject Maths. He just had fun in his chemistry periods with Koma.

The routine at Krya was this, Surya would first go to Krya, he'll be waiting for Koma to come, Later when he came, and he and Surya would go to the canteen and just walk in the corridors. When the first bell strikes, he and Koma would enjoy the classes, both would hang out together, laugh together, and have fun together. Most of the time it was only Surya and Koma that hung out together. Jean had some more people to hang out with. She found her twin sisters eventually, who were as lazy as her. Yet, Koma, Surya and Jean would never miss any phone calls each day Especially Surya and Jean during the computer exams. It was Surya who taught Jean every concept of computer science subject. It was one fine day when Surya was speaking with Jean, about Priyanka.

"Yes, everybody thinks she and I are in some sort of crush! But she and I are just friends!" Surya said to her.

"Is that so? Then tell me one thing Surya... How do you think news like these spread?" Jean asked.

"There are a lot of jobless people who're bored in this world J."

"Yeah...? So how many boys are there in your old school?"

"I never did head count J."

"Well, let's assume there are 300 boys, alright?"

"Okay..."

"From the 300, why were you alone chosen huh?"

"Mm...! Because, only I speak with her."

"What about the guy you call Krishna?"

"Yeah he too... Well, he speaks much more than me."

"So, then why wasn't he chosen, Surya?"

"Look, why should all of you think in the same way? Can't we be just friends?"

"We all say it that way because we realised this that way...! Alright? She is having some feelings over you!"

"But... but..." Surya gasped.

"Leave it Surya! I know girls right? We can't hide our feelings for long. Come on she was a friend to you in childhood, it's teenage! Everything changes. How many times do I have to tell this to you Surya? Don't make her wait. You might've loved Shivani, but you can't miss someone who truly loves you, Surya. Understand this and don't make her wait for so long. Don't give her the disappointment you had from Shivani."

"Keeping this as a chance, you're telling me to believe you are a girl huh? Okay let's take your advice once. Let me think over it, if she's strong on her crush, if she really has one."

"You stupid, while I'm helping you're teasing me huh...? Idiot. Anyways, good luck for tomorrow's practical exam Surya!"

"Okay... bye..." Surya cut the call from the phone, and then saw a notification for a text message. It was from Priyanka. He started looking over for it. While he was looking over it, he thought about what Jean said. Over the last few days, Surya and Koma spoke about Priyanka. Everybody thought Surya and Priyanka were in a relationship.

It was one fine day in August, when there was nearly a fight between Koma, Jean and Surya. What Surya felt was friendship and what the other two thought was different. It was Koma who was telling in every angle that Priyanka was having a crush over Surya. It was on that day, Surya wanted to test whether what they said was true.

Surya was sitting on the bus. He was on his way to home. Surya and Nandhu were sitting in the second row. Surya told Nandhu about the things Koma said. So, Surya wanted him to check for whether Priyanka was seeing him or not. Nandhu turned to look back.

"I don't know dude, who's that Priyanka?" Nandhu asked.

"The fairest girl in the bus, with a curly hair, not too tall, not short too."

"We can't see a person's height while they're sitting, genius."

"Okay, try to find her."

"Yup, found her. Does she blink a lot?"

"Yeah I think so." Surya said, looking forward to pretend as if he wasn't noticing.

"If that's the girl, I think she's watching you even now."

"What!"

"Yep...! I'm sure. She's watching you right now!"

"Oh boy...! She's pulling me to keep the test."

"What test?"

"I've thought about asking this issue to her indirectly. If she replies favour to it, there's nothing I can do."

"You're not making any sense to me."

"*I can make some sense, but you'll be going to your home only half an hour later, is that okay?*" *Surya said; pointing outside where Nandhu's stopping had come.*

"*Aw crap...! Alright, all the best with the test, buddy!*" *Nandhu said laughing.*

After Nandhu got down, it was Surya's stop next. Surya was packed ready. As the bus stopped with a squeaking sound, Surya looked back. He saw Priyanka getting up. He got up first and started getting off the bus. Each and every day, Surya would rush to his cycle and would leave the stopping immediately. Surya never liked to speak with any of Priyanka's friends, eventually he wouldn't speak with Priyanka or Nisha when they both come with them but today he decided to stay. He started speaking with Priyanka and Nisha.

"*Hey guys! Long-time no see!*" *Surya said to both.*

"*Hey!*" *Both of them replied.*

"*So, Surya, what's up?*" *Nisha asked.*

"*Nothing Nisha, Just wanted to see my old friends.*"

"*Old friends huh?*" *Nisha imitated.*

"*Yes, we're old friends to him Nisha, he's got new ones right...? Especially people from abroad.*" *Priyanka said.*

"*Now, come on. It's just a figure of speech. So, how's school for you two?*"

"Hmmm, well guess what, we both are in the toppers list. We get special coaching each weekend. They are bringing special teachers to help us with the subjects." Nisha added.

"Toppers? But, quarterly term exams aren't up yet? How'd they...?"

"Oh, Surya we have cycle tests right, for 30 marks every last week of the month?" Nisha said

"Yeah, even I have them. It's for no use. They just keep them for namesake."

"NO! You don't know. Ask any people who got first marks in them. They would've been called for those classes as well. I've seen CBSE guys' class as well." Nisha added.

"What?"

"Yes Surya. They're actually a small performance tests." Priyanka said. She had trouble in telling this.

"So..." Surya cleared his throat and continued. "So, I don't have to say my status in school then. I don't even know about this."

"Surya, be pleased that you escaped. We literally forgot the term holiday!"

The friends walked silently for a few minutes in the road. Surya had been really mocked on hearing about the special classes. It was then, it hit in his head that he's got studies much more to do than anything else. Surya had been speaking to Priyanka for a few days.

He recollected asking her about her studies and all she said was it was tough and she couldn't cope up with them. When Surya said that his difficulty was in chemistry alone, she too voted yes for it and she told him that chemistry was the subject she could never learn. On the whole, all that she told him was that she had a lot of tough times and scare towards studies and she really can't cope up with them. Now, hearing that she's one among the toppers, Surya felt both happy as well as sad.

Priyanka had hid from him the fact of her being the topper. If she really had a crush on Surya, she would've told him about it, in the fact of at least sharing her happiness with him. When Priyanka was not even ready to share this simple thing, how in the heavenly world would she be having crush over him? This logic gave him happiness. But, it couldn't last long. The fact of her being among the toppers triggered his mind to think about him to be the topper. There was a pressure in him. He had to be among toppers, but his entire stand now is that he not even knows that the school had already recognised the toppers and they're now getting an even more better coaching than him. He's been missing the play for a long time. At least now, to get hold to reality, Surya wanted to know what all they're getting as toppers. Yet, he was little disappointed at himself for not making up to the topper stage. So, he decided to leave the topic. Then, Nisha's house was the first one they came to. From there Nisha departed and Surya and Priyanka were walking towards their home.

"I'm sorry I didn't tell that matter to you Surya." Priyanka said slowly.

"No! Don't mention it. I'm okay with that." Surya said. His voice sounded low with the thoughts that were running in his mind to get to the topper scale, which Priyanka thought him being mad at her.

"I'm really sorry Surya. You told you did not like chemistry and maths right? I didn't want you to feel lonely about the case. That's why I too didn't say I belong to the topper category."

"Not a problem… I'm not worried Priyanka, I just am thinking about something else." Surya said, to which Priyanka's imagination grew every second. She at the moment burst out.

"Please don't be silent Surya. I cannot be happy if you aren't. I think we need to share the happiness and sadness together! I can't be happy when you're sad!" Priyanka said.

Surya at once got into his senses. He asked Priyanka,

"What did you say?"

"I can't be happy if you are not. My happiness is valuable only with you!"

"That's a lot of words Priyanka! We're just friends! You'll find an even more valuable person than me soon in your life."

"Yes I may, but I can't lose you too Surya can I?"

"Alright, let's chop off the topic. You know, today was the real fun in my class. I just realised something." Surya started with a topic, or to be precise, he started his test.

"Yeah...? What's that?"

"I am the youngest boy in our batch! I may be even younger than you!" Surya said. His 'big' idea was to check whether Priyanka was getting sad or not when she finds out Surya being younger than him. That's the basic need in a couple to him, for the boy being older than her. To his idea, he thought, as he was born on 21st of May 1996, he was placed in the batch where students of 1995 were studying, due to the academic year difference. So, he thought telling this to Priyanka, he can find whether she is in love with him, as when he's younger she'd definitely feel it bad to have feelings for him and those will be reflected. And when she's happy, taking it as a good joke, she's not having any feelings over him.

"Yeah...? What's your date of birth?" Priyanka asked.

"21st May 1996" Surya said proudly, but yet, with a cautiousness to look in Priyanka's expression. To his surprise, Priyanka started laughing. Surya successfully got the good result of the test. 'She's not having a crush over me. She's taking this lightly! She's still only friend to me! Wow! Nice!" Surya thought to himself. But... just then,

"I'm the youngest Surya! I was born on 11 august 1996! Sorry to burst your bubble Surya!" Priyanka spoke and started laughing even more.

Surya's smile evaded. Now, he's not in a mood to ask abruptly his question. Yet, he was desperate to know the truth. Surya was so impatient. He now doesn't know why she's laughing. Is she laughing because I got fooled or I'm being elder than her? Is this a laugh of fun or a laugh of satisfaction? Surya didn't know. His question now had a hypothetical answer. Surya shook his head and thought let time decide this and bid bye to Priyanka after a few minutes and started to leave for his home.

Later as days passed, Surya too started noticing. Surya found her texts extremely caring. Surya was feeling really good. At least now, someone cared for him, and he really wanted this. Yet, those times Surya thought it was a good friendship what Priyanka had in him. But, when Koma and Jean told him about all these, his mind began to deviate from the focus. Surya was so confused. When he tried to test whether what Priyanka had in him even later, it always looked towards crush and not friendship. Surya began to feel that Priyanka liked him. It always put a smile in his face on thinking of this. It was making him feel better. It made him feel to prove that he was a better guy.

Now, we've been so hung up on August, let's get to September. Today, after speaking with Jean, Surya had a text message from Priyanka. It read,

'All the best for tomorrow's exam, do come and tell me that you wrote it well. Good night, sweet dreams and take care!'

When Surya was about to reply for the message, he heard his father calling him. So, suddenly he went inside.

"Tomorrow you've got practical exam right?" Surya's dad asked.

"Yes daddy, tomorrow both computer science and chemistry practical"
Surya replied.

"Have you prepared?" His father asked.

"Yes daddy, computer science is very easy! Yet chemistry only is
scaring me."

"If it's scaring, concentrate more in it. That's all I can say. You're
not a small child to spoon feed you. You know what to do, we've got
expectations in you and we've invested a lot in you. These are the first
exams in your new school. Do well."

Surya got a little chill inside him. That's not because of his father's
words, but the phrase 'Investing money' involved in the chill. Surya
was always freaked on the money topic as he really knew the money
that was poured on to the cost of education Krya gives. Surya was
determined to do his work yet fear of failure always scared him. Surya
continued to his level, and he still didn't achieve much to expectations.
And the topics of special classes, average marks for hard works in his
tests started scaring him more. When he's planting a step, the sands
slide away from him, for which the scared mind don't dare to keep the
step afterwards.

His fear built day by day and the only way it had to stop was to smell
success. Yet, Surya couldn't smell it even now. When he was in C.B.W.,
he had a lot of extra engagements that made him divert his mind and
put in good mood and achieve in different kinds of success. But now,
his life was concealed within the walls of the classroom in the day and

his bedroom in the nights. Not a good environment for a student like Surya. He would want a little diversion from everything time to time. For the record, every human being would need them too, depending on the people who learnt to adapt to the environment, which our boy Surya has not yet learned.

Chapter 25: Face the failure.

*W*hen do we all pray God…? Some of us every day; some every hour; some for nearly all the time, after certain age. God is our hope. God is our trust. When we feel we can't do anything, we then seek God. He's our guide. We remember to scold him when we don't get something; we forget to thank him whenever he's gifting us. Perhaps, humans always are attracted towards negative things, than praising the positive ones. We can't forget something bad a person commits. We get reminded of the action whenever the person passes by. Whereas when we see good things, when we see people do good things, they're just a painting that's going to be washed in the swirling waters of life.

Surya was really gifted to join in Krya. He was actually let into the field of tigers to practise survival. It's a place where a higher competition is being conducted. People of higher ranks played in it. Surya, who was good in the lesser level competition, has gone to the next level. Well, only thing to notice is, he had failed to realise that he has to perform, rather than hating the level of heat that's been given to him. He has to fight in the arena, where he just watches in 'awe'. While he watched, his rival had come. The challenges as exams had to be met. Well, the challenge might be easy. It's too easy to survive, and far more difficult to win in this life. The winning takes us somewhere high, but the device that we need to take us there, is in *our hands. No success comes at its wish. It had to be pulled down to ground through hard work.*

Well, Surya wasn't strong enough to pull. He's weak, and he wasn't ready yet, which made him face three blows in Krya. The three blows that might have been avoided, but had to hit to make a strong impression on Surya's mind deep down; an impression necessary to understand to jump through and hunt down the jungle of dangers, called life. These three blows will strike through Surya; through his heart. It would produce him a trailer for what the real world is like. It would show him how the people are performing in the world to achieve big things. It would show what the society is made up of and it would show him, how bad times may change a person. These three blows may happen in everyone's life. Yet, they happened so fast in Surya's life, which God had decided to place them one after the other. This is going to be a rough ride for Surya, as there won't be any help he'll get, for when he gets, he might fail to learn God's lesson.

The day of practical examinations had started to the eleventh graders. Surya and Koma were at the corridors of the computer lab. They were busy. They couldn't pay attention to any outside interactions. They weren't even looking to their left or right sides. They just bent their heads down and Surya and Koma were deeply concentrating on it. Surya had his book in his hands. They didn't utter a sound. Only then, Jean came by. She saw the boys so still and silent, looking down something at their hands. She thought for them reading so silently and cautiously that they didn't even make any sound. She went near them and asked.

"What are...?" Jean asked but suddenly Surya shushed her. She got irritated and turned Koma by his shoulder. When he turned, a round, blue bug with orange stripes flew away from Koma's hands.

"What the..?" Jean paused.

"Ohhh!!! It flew away!!!! J! I told you to keep quiet! That's a bug we never saw! We wanted to keep it! I and Koma struggled a lot to get it into our hands! And you from the Emirates took it away from us!" Surya said.

"Fools! Don't you remember that the exam's in about ten minutes!?"

"Yea, I remember! So what? Shouldn't we take a look at a bug?" Koma asked

"Have you prepared?"

"Yes! Come on! It's just C++"

"Oh yeah? So then maybe you could help me with the sorting problem!"

"What sorting problem?"

"The program to sort a set of numbers in arranging order."

"We have a program like that?!"

"Great! Now stumble upon your book and Surya why are you so quiet today? Break up with Priyanka?" Jean asked.

"Yea right, as if we've been in relationship for years!" Surya said.

"Who knows? Maybe!" Koma said, looking at his notebook and smiling.

"You bloody cr..." When Surya came to speak, suddenly Mrs Preethi came through the corridors. While she came, she saw Surya, Koma and Jean and said,

"Oh, you've come early! Such an interest to write the test eh?"

"No ma'am, not even a single drop of interest towards the test to me." Koma said, smiling.

"Well, that's good then. Don't write the test, I need an assistant to conduct the test."

"Then full marks if I do that ma'am?"

"Yes, for an assistant. For Koma... zero. As he'll be absent for the test."

"Oh! As the assistant is suffering from fever he won't be coming ma'am. So put him a zero and me, Komalesh a full present ma'am!" Koma said

"As if that's any better." Surya and Jean laughed on Mrs Preethi's comment.

Mrs Preethi entered the classroom and prepared the materials required to continue the test, while the students too started coming by. Then in about five minutes they were seated in their respective seats allocated in the lab. Surya got a seat with number 33, where Jean and Koma sat in the chairs 24 and 19 respectively. Koma and Surya were in the opposite ends of a same row and Jean sat at the row perpendicular to them.

"Students, the test comprises of two questions, both five marks each. If you show me the output for the programs you don't have to write them down in the paper. Else, you write and get it signed from me. And, no geniuses can see their adjacent computer for answers. The questions have different sets and no three adjacent people can have the same question. So better not do any handy-works alright?" Mrs Preethi said.

"Hmmm, as if I'll pass even if I copy." Koma said. "Hey you! If you get an easy question, can you give me your paper?" He tried to make a deal with a boy near him.

The boy next to him gave a frowned look and said, "Shut up stupid!"

"I'll see how you'll pass this test!" Koma said.

"Shh! What're you two speaking? Want to leave?" Mrs Preethi asked.

"Please don't make me sit next to him ma'am! He's asking me to give my paper if any easy question comes!" Koma complained against the boy.

"Koma... that's enough. All of us know what would have happened. Keep quiet." Mrs Preethi said and the test started by distributing the question papers.

Koma looked at Surya. Surya was stuck to his computer. He looked at Jean. She was looking at the question paper still, maybe thinking about what to write. Then, Koma looked at his question paper.

"Huh!! Sorting problem... Jean already told me to read this. I should've listened. Okay, let's see the second question... Oh my God! Matrix Multiplication! Surya told me to read this! I should've listened to him too!" Koma spoke to himself desperately.

"What Koma? Full marks this time?" Mrs Preethi asked.

"Yes ma'am definitely! These are very simple questions ma'am! I'll write it even when I'm asleep!" Koma boasted himself.

"Then why the sad look in your face before I asked Koma?"

"I pitied my condition to write such a simple test as this ma'am!" Koma said.

"Then come, I'll give you another question paper! Don't worry!"

"No, No! My friends will feel inferior to match my level! Let it be there ma'am!" Koma said. Though he boasted, his heart was weeping to have not studied the two programs. He looked to his left and right. He saw that his question paper was marked with the number 6. He looked at the number to the right of him. He saw it as 1. So, he started counting to find who has the set number 6. Luckily, in the 'H' shaped placement of the lab computers, he found the person with set 6 just beside him in the perpendicular row. So, all he did was thank God first, and then he started typing through the keyboard with his head turned left.

In about twenty minutes, Surya got up and left the lab. After a few minutes Jean went too. For Koma, he had to write the programs as he couldn't bring the output, he took the whole period to finish the test. Later, when he went out, he saw Surya and Jean waiting for him.

"So, what set?" Jean asked.

"6" Koma replied.

"... and the questions were?" Surya asked.

"Sorting and Matrix multiplication." Koma replied with his head bent low.

"Ahem, ahem." Jean cleared her throat.

"Okay! I get it! You told me to read that and you want to say 'I told you so' right? Please move!" Koma shouted at them and went.

Both Surya and Jean went and spoke with Koma. They just joked with him and were getting down the stairs to get to the chemistry lab.

"So... Surya! How was exam for you! You went first! Didn't you know anything?" Koma asked.

"No, I finished the programs. All of them... got outputs, so ma'am told me not to write the code. So I came fast!" Surya said.

"You backstabbing bat!" Koma told and continued, "I never knew you could read!"

"Ahem, come on man! Be serious! These are exams! We have to be serious!" Surya said.

"Yeah, yeah, buzz off!" Koma said and went to drink water.

"So Surya, really, how was the paper?" Jean asked.

"Really it was damn easy J. I knew I could do well. Yesterday was freaked out about exams. But now I think I can handle these. I really feel happy. I might get a centum. For the first time feeling that centum sensation! Phew!" Surya spoke as his eyes glowed with happiness, happy to feel the exams being easier on him. He felt the terror driven away. He was now not running from the fear that had struck him. With this same happiness, he went to the Chemistry lab. The place is where God's going to land the first blow.

"Good evening, ma'am." Every student in the chemistry lab wished to Mrs Nancy, for she came with a bundle of papers and threads in her hands.

"Good evening students." She replied and kept those papers and went to speak on with Mr Durai, the lab attendant. After a few minutes, she announced.

"Every biology group students come to my left and the computer students come to my right."

As she ordered, nearly the class was separated into two groups and were placed on to their streams respectively as Mrs Nancy said. "Look students, the whole class will be split into two. The first group would be given the salt and would perform the test and write the observations later and the second group will be asked to get out of the lab, sit in the class just beside us and write the experiments' tests and would do the experiments when the first group finishes. Now, as there are more biology students, first you people go and start writing while the other group finishes the tests."

After she said, the biology students took a paper to themselves and got out of the lab. The computer students stayed. As per the roll numbers, they were given separate tables to perform the experiments. Surya sat at the second platform on the second row. Just next to the teacher's desk.

Surya sat with nervousness. He felt he can do the test. His thoughts were this: Oh my God, last night I stayed up till three to write this test. I read nearly all of the material, first colour and appearance, then solubility, then flame test, then ash test, then… Ohhh, why can't I remember what's next! What's after ash test! Okay, let me wait. When I get the salt I'll remember. I'm thinking too much. Let's wait. My portion had… Calcium Carbonate, Sodium Chloride, Sodium sulphate, Potassium Hydroxide, wait, are these really salts? Oh my God! What's happening! Okay, let's calm down for God's sake!

Then in a few minutes, Durai Sir came and started distributing the salts. He was smiling at the boys while he gave. Some boys even dared to ask him about what salt, to perform the testing of acid and basic radicals directly, that is the final step of the experiment. But, all Durai sir did was just smile at them and pass on to the next boy. He saw Surya and spoke with a big smile!

"Hey Amul baby! Here, I'll give the easiest salt for you! Do well!" Durai sir said with a good smile in his face, he gave a blue coloured *salt to Surya. Surya looked at it. He completely forgot what will be a blue coloured salt. He looked at the people, beside and in front of him. Everybody got a white coloured salt, whereas he's the only one who had the blue salt. He thought to himself, 'The easiest salt and I couldn't write it!' He looked and looked around. Everyone did something with their salt. A boy took a test tube, mixed the salt with water, added some solutions to it, put it above a Bunsen burner, noted down the experiment. Another boy, took the salt, made it into a paste with some solution, took a big tube that had a cork, inserted it into the test tube, took water in the jug, put it above a tripod stand, inserted the other end of the tube inside water and in a few minutes, the water turned yellow with the smoke from the tube, then there was a girl, who took the salt in a test tube, took a solution from a bottle and just when she poured few drops, the salt inside burst up with huge effervescence and popped out of the test tube as a volcano. Everybody did this and everyone took their observations quickly, while Surya watched all these as a magic show, with his fellow students as magicians. It all happened so fast.*

Whenever Surya encountered a progress of the student, he felt scared. What they did, and what he saw was no miracle but pure simple science, but he couldn't understand it. He couldn't do it. This was the fear that had come. This fear geared up in his spine, made it cold, his heart froze. What was happening around him fed the fear in him. His visions were blocked, his thoughts locked, brain stopped and his adrenaline pumped. He couldn't get a grip onto himself. His chariot of fear went and attacked his whole body. The fear of incompetence, the fear of inability, the fear of failure, killed his cells and tissues of the body. Students finished their experiments and went outside and the students of the first group came in as everyone went. Time never waits is what we already know. Each time the clock ticked, fear hammered Surya's heart. Each time a person entered, he left his confidence. Each time a student submitted the paper and went, he saw himself drown, while the world happily passed by him.

Till now, he tried and tried to remember something that he read, something that was so easy while he was at his home, something that minutes before seemed so easy, yet, he was denied of it. Surya's fear taunted him more as he fell to its prey. Surya was never going to come back out of this for a long time. It's no use to fight back now. It's all over. He had bid the confidence a bye, that's gone so long now. But, this is now off the level than it was supposed to be. God isn't that cruel, if he was, he wouldn't be God. So, on making Surya realize the lesson, he wished to offer some help, and that is, through the person called Mr Durai.

"What happened, Surya...? You haven't written even a word! Why?" He asked seriously.

"Sir... Sir... I couldn't..." Surya's voice broke. He couldn't speak. The chill he had in the spine and heart, seized his vocal chords, that didn't allow him to speak.

"Okay no time to speak now. Mrs Nancy is gone to the other room, where the children are writing the exam. Not many students are here

too. Wait, I'll tell you what this salt is; write what you know about it. I'll help you." Durai sir said.

"Thank you sir! Thank you Sir!" Surya said and inhaled deep and cleared his throat and wiped off the small tears that came through the eyes of the fear and jotted down the pen.

"Now, the salt is..." Mr Durai started explaining him what the salt was and what are the experiments for it. He told the basic five experiments and went aside to bring the test tubes that contained the finished tests of the similar salt done by another student. Surya was so thankful to him that he smiled through the tears just for Durai sir. But, before his happiness could complete, his failure peeped. Before he could finish the whole experiment, Mrs Nancy came.

"Sir, all completed there, let's arrange the..." Mrs Nancy was surprised to see Surya to be there in the lab still.

"Surya! What are you still doing! Everybody Left! Look at the time! Its ten minutes past bell! Didn't you leave? You have bus to catch also right?"

"Oh my God! Yes ma'am the bus will leave in five minutes!"

"Then what are you doing till now! If you couldn't do the experiment you could've told me right? I would've helped you! This isn't board exams anyway!" Mrs Nancy said. This triggered Surya's emotions more and more! He cursed himself for his stupidity. Mrs Nancy came towards him nearly running, the bus trip was to start and if a student

misses it, he must go through a private transport and the teacher would be blamed for the stay of the child. So, she came in rushing towards him and plucked away the paper from him and said,

"Go, Surya, these are just quarterly, let's do it later, nobody gives preference to these exams. Go now! Than this boarding the bus is important! Go Go GO!"

Surya looked at the paper that ma'am took away from him. His first failure goes and he can do nothing about it. Surya then rushed outside the lab to take out the bag and unzipped it and pushed his items through them, didn't close them properly and ran to the gate outside. There, he saw bus number one before him with all its students already boarded and even the doors were closed. It came to thought to him that if this bus was closed, probably bus number 20 would've already departed! So, with his bag swaying from right to left, Surya jolted out through the main door of the school. He ran furiously. His heart pumped so fast. He felt his breathe getting heated and his legs getting weak. If he loses the bus, he'd probably end up calling his father, making him come. That too, he can't be staying within the campus. At least he had to stay near the security's station. He can't do that. When will his father come after the call? It'd take nearly an hour for him to even depart from I.E.C. campus. If he starts late, it'd be no less than nine o'clock for Surya to reach home. For that, a hard struggle to the bus now, is way better. So, Surya went panting to the bus, saw the bus nearly start with the shake and the conductor board and close its door, far away, for he was just crossing bus number 8 now.

The bus started and moved. Surya, only then, with all the power of his vocal chords and lungs, Surya shouted "STOP!" but the conductor couldn't hear it. The bus was still moving. Suddenly, Surya lost all his hope and started to stop. But, suddenly, fate was kind to Surya. A Physical training master suddenly showed up seeing Surya running and shouting. So, without hesitation he blew his whistle hard. His whistle was louder than Surya's voice, making the driver himself look into the rear view mirror and see Surya running towards the bus and stop the bus.

While Surya ran, he saw the master and thanked him. He, in return, just smiled and told him to board the bus fast. Surya went and finally boarded the bus. As he boarded it he saw Nandhu looking surprised at him and he looked back to find Priyanka looking relieved on seeing him. He didn't react much and was panting heavily. His mind was as tired as his body. Yet, the incident of him looking at his paper, surely knowing that he'd fail for the first time in his life, played again and again in his head as he blankly watched the passing world outside the bus, feeling and cultivating the terror again and again.

Chapter 26: What is Love?

*T*he day Surya got his first blow stroke him hard to the ground. People have advised us through many phases of life. They had told, "If life pushes you down, you can choose whether or not to get up." Well, what was the case in Surya's life was that, he never knew he could get up. He felt he was pushed into a deep well, without any means to come up. He was so afraid to look up his subjects again.

Whenever he studied, he just read what was there in his books, while his mind played with his failure. Remember a fight with Surya's brain and heart when he was in A.K.R.S.? When he went on to see the game in the P.S.P. that he forgot to tell other kids' parents to call his parents and tell them to call him? Well, the fight got severe now. He was having a fight to realize his ability and hold on to his dreams and hope. His heart hoped that he'd better himself up and would succeed, whereas his mind reminded the failure and stroke down the confidence. When a fight goes in within, how could peace be generated and how could the boy read? Well, obviously he couldn't and what Surya faced till now was failure.

This was one night where Surya was furiously reading Chemistry theory questions. This is the 29th of January 2012, Sunday night. Surya has a test on the next day in the first period. Surya just then, had a fight in him on the same issue even now. An incident happened just few minutes before.

"What do you think Hari? He's not providing any results to me! He's failed in chemistry and maths the two terms and in physics he barely passed! Only in computer and English he's getting good marks! I don't know if he has any fear towards studies anymore!" Surya's dad spoke to his brother inside the bedroom, with Hari and Surya's mom sitting beside, whereas Surya overheard the conversation outside the closed door.

"I don't know Pa, He studied well in C.B.W. don't know what's happening in this school." Hari said.

"But, he's reading all the time inside his room! He never comes out as before! He simply sits and reads loud!" his mom said.

"You don't defend your son! It's no use to him! If you have to scold sometimes, you have to do it! That's our duty! Just because he's our son, doesn't mean he's always doing right things alright!" his dad's voice got high.

"No dad, don't scold mom! She's right! Surya does sit and read all the time! I myself had seen him do so!" Hari said.

"Then where are the results?" his dad asked in frustration.

"Maybe the syllabus is really tough dad! Don't you know many had told us that CBSE syllabus was really tough in 11th and 12th grades?"

"Yes, but how long can it go like this? When other kids read, why can't my son?"

"He's not a dumb boy dear." His mom said.

"Yes dad, he got good marks before right?" Hari said.

"I know he's not a dull student. He got good marks before, but why he couldn't get them now is my question."

"Keep your voice down dear, he could hear!" his mom said.

"Alright. Okay, all I feel is this. I have invested a lot of money in educating him now. It's been half an academic year and till now everything is at its worst. If this goes on, there's no way for me, but to pay donation in a college as I pay in this school. Sums and sums of money I'll pay and will join him. That's the best I can do. I can only take the horse to the river. I can't make it drink. If he wakes up now and read well knowing the fear of life, he'll escape. Else, he'll be suffering along with us. Now everybody get some sleep. Company's getting as hell as it could be and life's at hell too. Don't know what we'll reap in this God forsaken life." Surya's dad said desperately and went off to sleep.

That moment, Surya felt helpless in his life. He felt that he's at a sinking ship. There's no good thing that he could do anymore. He felt he's all trapped deep down and he's going to face only failure hereafter. The life has changed and all he had done ended up in constant disappointments. He left off his final hold of confidence.

His family felt the way he had felt about himself. He's turned out to be a failure and Surya's dad's mentioning about the failure again and again stabbed his heart repeatedly. His fear grew as an ocean within himself and was making his very own existence heavy. All Surya did that day was sat silently before God in his room and then looked on to his notes without any hope of learning.

"Surya!" Hari called.

"Yes! Coming!" Surya replied and went.

"Dad and I were speaking about you just now."

"Yeah I heard." Surya replied.

"You heard right? Then tell me what the problem is? Why are you failing these days? What's happening in that school?" Hari asked. Surya remained silent.

"Look Surya, Dad has invested a lot in you. I was the one who disappointed him first remember? Remember the day my board exam results came?" Hari asked Surya as Surya's eyes widened in the past horror memory.

It was May '08. Surya's brother Hari had completed his 12ᵗʰ grade and was waiting for the public exam results. When the whole family saw his brother's marks, Surya's dad went furious. The mark of the son was disappointing to Surya's dad. Things like marks meant a lot for Surya's dad. He always dreamt of saying the whole world proudly the marks of his son. That too, his greatest expectation was on the first son. The first time the family member had written a public level exam and who doesn't have curiosity to know what that was. So, with that level of expectation, Surya's family watched the disappointing results of Hari. Thunder struck in the family that day, for Surya's dad for the first time cried so furiously, ashamed to face the people who'll be asking the marks of his son, threw the pictures of Gods from the room, cursing them for not showing mercy towards the family. His mom too was worried heavily. Surya's brother looked on to his dad's pain and mourned. While young Surya was scared to death of the family's unusual behaviour. That day was a nightmare in Surya's memory. Each and every second Surya lived there, he felt startled and scared.

When Hari mentioned about that day, Surya's mind felt heavy, his neck wringing, stomach gurgling. That's the most fear Surya got. Later on Surya's thoughts went on with the day in May '08. He placed himself in Hari's situation. He could never even face that kind of scrutiny. Surya was startled. Well, Hari then left off the conversation after few minutes. He thought Surya was cautioned, but he didn't know that Surya's frightened now. He's nearly scared to death. Later Surya thought about himself. He thought about the trouble he had given to the family. He thought about peace that the family once had, he thought about him taking away from it, and finally he thought about life. It was then, only then, Surya broke. He broke into tears. He tried to stand up, but fate smashed him hard to the ground. To him, he's crushed and there's no way out anymore. He's no good than a corpse that lay low in the ground. All he thought was, 'My life's gone!

There's no happiness! I'm as good as dead anyway!' That night Surya never moved. He stayed there, cried there and dozed off there as well.

The next day was the test on chemistry. Surya was sitting in his bench looking at a person. That person was laughing so happily. She was having a good time with her friends. Surya thought to himself. 'Where's my happiness gone? Is the world so scarce of happiness, that God took it from me and gave it to the world? If that's the cause he's really a reasonable person, else he's just a naughty millionaire's son, wasting my cost of happiness.' He shook his head and looked down.

Mr Ram came with the question papers. The test was on Chemical bonding. Surya didn't study yesterday; anyway it wouldn't be much of importance even if he did. He couldn't have made much improvement. Surya waited calmly for the question paper, he got it. As he thought he didn't know many answers. He looked at the paper, circled the questions that he think he knows and that he can write and calculated how much marks he might get. He crossed the passing marks. He felt nothing and he wrote what he knew. Meanwhile the one sitting next to Surya was Ajay. He looked at him using two pens, one to highlight and other for answers. He was so busy nearly decorating the paper with perfect beautiful answers. Surya saw how good his answering method was. Than learning from it, he compared to his and got disappointed. Than trying out his techniques he praised it and cursed himself for not doing it. He was in whole disappointment of himself. He was no longer hoping that he could survive this place. While these thoughts lingered he forgot to divert his vision, and Ajay saw him looking at *his paper directly. He said, "What dude? Is this good? Why peeping like a rat? This is an easy test. You could've read right?"*

Ajay's intention was good. He advised him well. But, Surya got furious. He thought that Ajay was showing off that he's advising him now. His anger rose high. A man is always a king to himself. No man likes much of advice from a fellow man. It's a thing that gets on the nerves for the present condition of Surya. He was as like a bomb that could explode anytime. He was as fragile as glass at the moment. Koma looked at Surya. Koma saw Surya change drastically from the chemistry lab exams during quarterly. He asked what the matter was the next day yet he couldn't find any solution to Surya. Days past bad after the first blow Surya got. He behaved as a bull that without any plans just ran into the red cloth shown. He just thought that marks were the one and only goal he needs and did a barbaric job in study. He just ran through the topics again and again than understanding them on the go. If that be the case, how in any world would a boy get knowledge and a good study?

The path that Surya went was very destructive. He closed himself into a black box thinking that it was the only solution to him to achieve success. He stopped texting anyone, he never called anyone, and he practically cut off the whole connections to the outside world. Seeing this behaviour of Surya, his friends reacted in a different way. Koma tried to cheer him up as he could, but Surya wouldn't let him do so. Whatever practical jokes Koma came up with, Surya frowned upon it killing Koma's interest too. Jean spoke too, how much could anybody help, when the person in need doesn't allow it too? So, friendship with Jean began to deteriorate as well. Surya once when desperate, went on to play too, but everybody played Soccer or Basketball in Krya which is very unlikely not Surya's game. Surya was shut down the door to sports and physical fun with them that day. He couldn't even kick the ball when it came to him.

You may think… just one incident and all the world gets upside down? Imagining ourselves in a situation of him, getting failed in the fields of academics, games, public relations, respect, even peace from the family, we would end up in a lot of frustration making the world a living hell. When the step we keep buries down everywhere, we would really end up standing in the same place than reach for any other, with friends or success or goals. This burned up Surya's mind. He once lost part of his carefree smile in A.K.R.S. he left it to the whole in Krya. He always looked somewhere, thought something, heard nothing and killed every joy he got. Perhaps, he reacted so much to one failure. God needed him to face failure, but not at this cost, maybe. So, there came an oasis in the desert. The water with palm tree must be so precious to continue the journey throughout the desert again. There God tried to heal Surya.

"Hey Surya!" Priyanka came in to the bus, where Surya alone was sitting simply gazing outside the window.

"Hi" Surya said silently.

"What's happening to you Surya? You're acting as if you're sick, you're so solemn and alone all the time!"

Koma came in to accompany Surya, but waited for Priyanka to speak to him. He thought Surya needs something good now. So he waited and heard what's going on inside the bus.

"Nothing Priyanka, Life's bizarrely gone down the hill to me. You know right, what goes up must come down? Well, it really is coming down."

"Come on Surya! There's no way that can happen! What I remember about you is, you were always joyful, remember your good times when you wore the sari in front of 31 schools? Remember how fabulous you got in that skit? How it made you get selected to the annual day celebration skit? Where's the smile that you plant in your face huh? You planted hilarious laughs to us those times Surya! Every guy in the audience crowd laughed at your jokes!" Priyanka said.

"Yes, think God too laughed at me. I'm sure he laughs now more than before." Surya said.

"You think you're having problems only now? Well, if I don't remember well, I couldn't tell you this incident. Remember when you acted in the play as the funny kidnapper, you forgot to bring the food to the small boy in the plot. Everybody asked you the food in the stage, you faced problem even there. If I was there I would've stammered and would've just run off through the scene. But what did you do? Do you remember?" *Priyanka asked. For the first time in weeks, Surya smiled. He got hold of the memory of the play. This brought joy to him.*

"YES!" *Surya shouted, for once his voice was high, he continued.* "I immediately asked the other boy who kidnapped, the food, he got hold to the scene and asked the other, like passing the buck and finally it got directed to me, in the mean time I went off stage took the food and came and gave it to him in the scene! Everybody commented that was a good comedy then where all I knew was it was never in the script! HAHA!" *Surya said.*

"Wow, haven't seen that smile for days!" *Priyanka said.*

"My friend's an actor!" *Koma thought while he stood near the bus.*

"Remember Surya, nothing suits you more than your smile. Laugh at hard times they say, hold on to that thought! You look good when you smile, don't lose it. I don't know if it means more to you, but to me, it's all that I want! Alright?" *Priyanka said.*

"Way to go big boy, you're really lucky to have her among you! She did what I was trying for nearly four months! Well, only the mystery is, who is she to you, friend or much more?" *Koma thought.*

"Thanks a lot Priyanka, thank you for reminding me, who I am!" *Surya said.*

"Okay, you keep this good feeling and do smile a lot." *Priyanka said.*

"Okay, I'm going to go get some fresh air outside. Bye…" Surya said and got down the bus, while he saw Koma smiling at him. Surya too smiled at him warmly.

"Wow, good to see that in you my friend. I can't help but overhear you two speaking, and you big crook, you never told me you can act! Huh?"

"You dirt bag, you were here the whole time? Alright don't tell this to anyone alright?"

"Why? You want to continue your shitty life again? Now, do what I tell you. It's about time God made me realise about your talent. This is February right? By the first week of March we'll have our annual day celebrations here. Why can't you just go for the skit auditions? They're conducting that tomorrow!"

"You said that, why should I deny it? Let's go!" Surya said.

Koma was so very happy that his friend got back in the game and was really very happy for it. He with that happiness came to embrace Surya! Surya again jolted back. "Koma, no! Never!" he said. And Koma just smiled and left while the Physical Master blew his whistle hard.

"And Surya, about that topic we found mysterious, about what really is happening, whether it is 'L' or 'F', I accept, I too am not so sure now!" Koma said and went. He referred to the mystery of Priyanka, whether she loves him or whether it's just friendship, even Koma got confused, for Surya now he clearly know that it was just friendship, as

it was Priyanka's behaviour of being nice to everybody! And this too, is just normal to her. Well, who knows?

Surya boarded the bus and sat in his place. He saw children board the bus quickly. He waited for Nandhu to come and he too came a few minutes later,

"How come you came so soon?" Nandhu asked.

"I and Koma didn't play; we just came directly to the bus, as the period was games period." Surya said.

"Okay. So, how's it with the mystery of Priyanka?" Nandhu asked.

"Mystery is solved. I don't think she's having any affection towards me. She's like that to everyone! So, I'm not any chosen one!" Surya said.

"Good to hear! It saves a lot of troubles Surya! Be happy! So, Surya, you know to march right?" Nandhu asked.

"Yes, I can do, why?" Surya questioned.

"Haven't you noticed that our school still didn't conduct the sports day? Till February?"

"Oh my God! Yes! I totally forgot about this!"

"Yes, due to some managerial reasons, they didn't conduct it till now. Our Physical master just told it's going to be conducted in the week consecutive to the Annual day celebrations time. So, he's asking me to tell the students about it to prepare for the march past. So, can I write your name down?" Nandhu asked.

"Of course bro!"

"Alright!"

The bus started slowly and steadily out of the Krya campus. It went on the road pleasantly. Surya was telling Nandhu about Priyanka as he was curious on how he came to the conclusion of her being just friend. So, Surya was explaining the past events he had with Priyanka. Then after a few minutes, both the friends started on to speak about the march past event.

"You know, if you did good march past, there might be chances for you to become School Pupil Leader you know?"

"Really? How?"

"Our houses will perform the march past in batches. Each house master looks on to the people who will march very well. So, you might have a chance to be the SPL if you marched well. Actually that's the main job of the SPL. Plus you need to be giving speeches. If you prove that you aren't afraid of the stage, you can be easily getting selected as the SPL."

"I got no problems! I'm not afraid of the stage and I'm damn sure I can march well!"

"Then good luck Mr SPL!" Nandhu said laughing. Then his stop came by and he boarded down. Surya was thinking about the SPL topic. He fascinated of being so from small grades. He always thought that was cool to be SPL. He wanted to take up duties, and perform really well.

But, surely he never expected to be SPL of Krya. Surya with those good thoughts found a miracle too.

The bus slowly hurtled towards the I.E.C. bus stop. Surya packed his bags and got down. Just as he got down, he met a person face to face, he breathed heavily on seeing that person, that person too was shocked on seeing Surya. Surya's body started to shiver. His adrenaline pumped. Even in a million years he didn't expect this to happen. His whole body was flooding with the rapid speed of blood that passed through the veins furiously. He found his breathing become heavy, his total body acting weird, his fore-head sweated badly, he recognised the same effect on the person too. His eyes closed to calmed down, when he opened, he saw a feel of satisfactory surprise in the person's eyes as well. The person was quick enough to get into senses and turn away. Surya looked as if he was questioning through his eyes, "What why are you turning?" and he tried to search for the eyes that spilled eternal juices of love just seconds ago. Well, it's now too long to be hung up there, his voice choked, shoulders worn down, heart raced, and he felt the ultimate joy again. The wave of love burst out through Surya, for he had finally saw Shivani!

Both of them forgot what they had spoken just a year ago, Shivani too forgot about all that Dhanvita had told her about, and Surya didn't even remember anything else. But yet, none of them were ready to speak up. Surya and Shivani are not in the perfect place yet. Their day will come. That day, they both will shed pieces of love; sow the seeds of love that will surely grow up to shed shades of goodness in the whole world. They would hold hands together and symbolize love to the whole world. But, everything needs time. It's not the time for all these to happen, for after all, Surya has been in a bad phase until now. He must entitle success. He must hold a firm grip onto the ground to hold Shivani in his hands. Dreams of him being with her would be pleasant if the environment is pleasing. He should not be in any manner provide sorrow to her. So, finally Surya got back to his senses and started leaving the place. Once, after walking a few steps, Surya turned to see Shivani, to his surprise, she turned on to look at him. Whether what Surya saw was illusion or God's magic, Surya saw Shivani's looks signifying that she's waiting for him.

That moment Surya found out the confidence he had in him. Though he thought about the failure he got, he now got the bump to flip it around. Though he failed before, he now wanted to fight back. Though he was haunted by the fear again, he decided to stop and face it! There was new hope that was sowed into Surya. He cleared his mind. He now knew that though he failed, it doesn't mean it was on him. Maybe he was not the person who could read well, maybe he's something else or something more! That too, when he thought about the marks in different subjects, he found out that he's one among the toppers in Computer Science. 'Maybe I'm a computer scientist than a chemist! Why should I worry now?' He asked.

That question signified the farewell of the terror in the boy's mind. That question gave him a boost to try on something in life that may let him know who he really is and what was the purpose of his birth.

That moment, he thanked Shivani in his mind. 'Shivani, when just the look of you can change my whole direction of life, how lucky would I be if I had you by my side the whole life? Thank you! Thank you! Whatever happens, I will fight for you Shivani! I won't leave you in my life forever! Let anybody put a barrier around you. I'll burst them open for you. I now know you too still like me. I do now know that you never meant any word that you said. God had showed me to you to let me know that you were my only goal in life, you complete me! You are my destiny and I'm ready to face you soon, no matter life takes me where. I'll swim to you! Just let's wait for the time to ripe. The fate will be ours, and we'll join hands together in this journey! Thank God! Thank you for showing my destiny!' Surya said and he walked briskly to his home from the bus stop.

Chapter 27: Knowing the world

"Oh! Mr Hudson, how come you ended up here?" Jake said.

"I was following Mr Watson. He went over Cathedral Street, over Palace Avenue. Later some henchmen attacked me. I was taken over in a cab... then... I don't know I ended up here." Mr Hudson replied.

"Mr Hudson, I'm having a feeling that they know our operations. I think we need to abort the mission immediately."

"That nasty little rascal caught me! Ugh!"

"Calm down Mr Hudson! Don't worry! We'll get him soon!"

"I tell you Jake! This bloody job needs younger people, people like you! I should've retired ages before!"

"Don't be so vexed up Mr Hudson! I know you've seen more troubles than these!"

"Yes I did! But only now I feel these as nut jobs!"

"Alright Mr Hudson, let's do this one last job together and roll this out completely."

"I too think so. Have you reported to the HQ? They might be in need for some info by now!"

"I'm keeping them posted time to time. Last information was about your reports only. They too were satisfied with the progress. But, things don't stay the way they are in our business."

"STOP!" Mrs Susan said. Guessed where we are? It's the skit practice going on in the auditorium of Krya. The plot was a detective story with two heroes; One Jake and the other Mr Hudson. Jake was a young detective who looks upon the famous Cornelius Hudson, The biggest detective of that time, well, in the plot.

Auditions went well to our Surya the other day. At first he was chosen to do some secondary role, a small character. Surya was pretty okay with that. He didn't prove much to get a lead role. He had a plan. He thought of showing his acting skills during the play so that the teacher decides it later, to give him a lead. Things went on smooth during play rehearsals. Every last period of the day would be cut for them. Surya escaped most of his Maths classes. He escaped Mr Xavier's stern looks and was happy for it. Surya then as he planned got the lead role. That too, not because of talent, but because of a lazy guy who wasn't interested to attend the rehearsals. So, the crew teachers asked for people to volunteer for the lead role in the crew. But, only then Surya got selected, as he looked big, as an aged man now, to be selected for Mr Hudson.

So, all is well, everybody got what they needed and the play went on with the rehearsals well. Well, if all is well where's the blow? Well, as this is the second blow, it is not just an attack. It's a strategically planned move of God, to make Surya know about the real face of the society. *The world as we know isn't as beautiful as it looks. We humans can't identify ourselves with love. We are not that 'divine'. We're merely the worst among the animals. We're the worst among the species. Except the gift of mind, there's nothing humans possess. They just want their favourite people to be favoured. Maybe God wanted to show Surya the real face of the common people we interact with. After all, Surya even called the shopkeepers 'bro' even though they never interacted with him even as a customer. He never blamed anyone for anything. He was not even angry for Mr Philip who pushed away Surya from the badminton match two years ago. Well, maybe Surya had to be shown this. Surya had to be warned. So, let's see what happens...*

"Excuse me ma'am!" Jacob entered.

"Jacob! Why haven't you come for so many days?" Mrs Susan said.

"Ma'am my throat was infected! I couldn't even speak ma'am! I told James about this too ma'am! Didn't he tell you?"

"No, my son James always plays the damn game you installed in the computer. Why did you give that to him?" Mrs Susan laughed.

"OH, that game is really addictive ma'am, but when he finishes it, he'll lose interest ma'am don't worry."

"Alright Jacob. Ahem, Surya, I told you to stop right? Now, I want you to do me a favour, can you give the script to Jacob here please?"

"But... why ma'am?"

"He was the one who was selected for Mr Hudson Surya! Don't you remember?"

"Ma'am, I've been in the role for three days now! I've prepared the whole script. I'm not even looking at it now!" Surya raised his voice in anger.

"Now, look. What did I tell you in the first place? I asked who'd volunteer for the role, you came by, and I gave you the script. When did I ever tell you to memorize it? If you do that, that's not my fault! Now give the script to him and sit down!"

"This is not fair!" Surya shouted. By that time the head of Co-ordinator, Ms Anne, who is also Surya's physics practical faculty, came inside the auditorium.

"Surya! What's this behaviour?" she asked.

"Ma'am! This Jacob came just today, and he's asking the lead role as if it was his right and she's asking me to give away it so easily. What's the prize of my work ma'am?" Surya asked.

"Is this true ma'am?" Ms Anne asked the ma'am.

"Ma'am anyway we already selected Jacob for the role!"

"Okay, let's see both the boys' performance." Ms Anne seemed just.

Both the boys were made to enact a scene. Surya was first. He enacted it well. Later it was Jacob's turn. Jacob seemed to get struck in a place. His expressions weren't promising.

"*Umm Surya?*" *Mrs Susan called Surya. After Surya's performance, Ms Anne had to attend to a circular given to her. Ms Susan found this as a window to lift up Jacob's acting.*

"*Surya, how will you react to the dialogue at this time?*" *She asked kindly.*

Surya found her promising. Her voice seemed acceptable. So, Surya showed her his expressions. He enacted the scene again. That moment, that's when the worst happened. The second blow was this...

"*Jacob! Did you see how Surya did it? Now do it the same way so that Anne sees you!*" *She told.*

"*WHAT!*" *Surya was shocked to hear these words from a teacher. He saw her with envy. 'How pitiful a creature might be? She's risking the whole play just because he's in it? How cheap these actions are? This behaviour is worse than the water in the sewers. I don't want to work with people who're this bad! YUCK!' These were his thoughts. Than feeling cheated, Surya felt hatred towards the cheap behaviour of the teacher. Surya just walked away from the auditorium. When Ms Anne said she could arrange for any other role... Surya said, "I'm way beyond these people ma'am. So, no thank you."*

"*Things won't be the same Surya.*" *Ms Anne said. She was helpless against the powerful domination of Mrs Susan. So, she just thought, that she could help Surya later. That day, Surya went to class straight away. He though felt bad about coming off of the play, he knew something that day.*

Not all people are kind, Not all cheats, everybody wants the development of somebody they favour, we can't reach success with a readily built elevator, we must build the steps brick by brick, and only when we keep the last brick, we would realize that we built success and it's not something that we must pursue, it's something which we craft. It's not something that we look upon; it's something we make about. It's not already there to go and get, it had to be prepared with our fine hands. And to do that, we must know who we are and what our potential is and how it can be increased. Surya learned his lesson through the second blow.

"PARADE! HALT!" A boy shouted at the top of his lungs as the march past group that had seven files of boys and seven files of girls at a stop in the circular soccer field of Krya. As the Quattuor Domos of the C.B.W., The Krya CBSE as every other school for the record had four houses. All the colours of the houses were as nearly same as C.B.W. Red, Blue, Green and Yellow. The fun thing about Krya was that they had their names under the precious gems of the world. They were Ruby, Diamond, Platinum and Gold. Though they couldn't match the colours with the names much they coined, the house of ruby with red colour, diamonds with blue, Platinum with green and Gold with yellow. Whether it was co-incidence or not, Surya always in whatever school he goes, ends up in the yellow colour house.

So, coming to our story, the boys and girls in yellow were marching for the past hour, to and fro and through and out of the soccer field. Their legs shook the whole ground and nearly each and every grain of the sand might be replaced from its initial position. Not only the gold's but the whole four houses marched in the ground. Surya was gold whereas Koma was a diamond, funny to hear, but true fact. Koma was in another house, Surya and Koma were separated. Good for both of them to do the work. Surya was pretty determined to do the march past perfectly as he wanted to become the SPL and show the school who he really was and what he was capable of.

You might wonder what happened to the play after Surya came out. Well, the ship of the play sunk bad, with Jacob's lousy dialogues and bad acting. The parents who came for the cultural went out of the auditorium to the canteen, as they couldn't bear to stand the boring two hour play. Well, things achieved in a bad way, won't do much help, do they? Well, let's not boast upon Surya either. The play would've been a failure even if Surya was in it.

So, the next thing is the parade. Surya marched well. For the first time, his tallness ensured him to stay in the first file and present himself first. He looked confident and he marched confident as well. The march past also had co-ordinators too; of course they were the teachers of Krya. Luckily, Susan was not gold, but a ruby. Even more luckily, Ms Anne was a gold. So, Surya had a better chance of becoming the SPL as Ms Anne could support him, so, planning that in mind Surya went and spoke to Ms Anne about him, working hard to be SPL.

"Only march past can't make you SPL, Surya." Ms Anne said.

"What else ma'am?" Surya asked.

"You have to show that you must be capable to talk and you mustn't be afraid of crowds."

"I am capable of talking in front of the crowd ma'am!"

"Everybody can speak whatever they want to Surya. But, you need to prove you are much more than that. How will you do it?"

"If only I can get a stage now!" Surya cursed.

"I can arrange that to you... If you'd like." Ms Anne said.

"Really ma'am?"

"Yes, but only if you could assure me that you could take up the heat."

"I can ma'am! Please trust me!"

"Okay, I'll let you know in the right time."

"When ma'am? Please tell correctly ma'am!"

"The right time."

"Ahem... alright ma'am. I'll wait for 'The right time.'" Surya said.

The march past practice went as perfectly as said, and the sports day dawned on the date, 18 February 2012, Saturday. The day was as warm as a mid-day in May, and pumped the waters out of everybody. The students were lined up steadily and waited for the day's celebrations to be inaugurated. At first, the management people *at the stage were giving speeches about the school and its support to extra-curricular activities, which lasted nearly an hour.*

By eight, the drum stroke! The 'bang' signified the people to be ready and steady, for the streaking colours of the boys and girls would adorn the yellow sand ground, for they marched on with pride and liberty. Every student in every place on the herd held their skin firm and tight and wore their bodies as shields. Their sharp looks in their face looked as if a sword bore with shield was getting closer step by step, with swift and stubborn turns, forming the most beautiful arrangement ever made by nobody but mere children. Well, would Surya be noted in the whole herd? Would he get what he desired? Who knows? Maybe, maybe not...

Chapter 28: Project: SPL.

"Ma'am you called?" Surya said, as he was in the physics lab, where Ms Anne and few more children of the tenth grade. As Surya came to the lab, Ms Anne sent them out, as they must be feeling scared about the senior most student of Krya. Yes! Surya is in twelfth grade! Than the amusement of it, the frightening part of twelfth grade is important. If we look on to the black board in the lab, we may find that it's dated June 4, 2012, Monday. Surya was called to make him show himself potent to be the SPL. Ms Anne kept her end of the bargain. She made a stage for Surya, and that, was the Fresher's party 2012. The event that Surya participated with him as the fresher just the last year and with the efforts of Ms Anne he gets to conduct it this year. Surya was called to be informed about this.

"Surya! The time has come…" Ms Anne said.

"Really ma'am?" Surya asked in anxiety.

"Yes! You wished that you'd want a stage right. Well I'm giving you a whole event. It's all yours. The fresher's party 2012, this day next week is your event! You get to do it as the co-ordinator. Happy?"

Surya opened his eyes wide in surprise. He couldn't believe his own luck! He got the opportunity he's been dying for! He just widened the smile more and more and more and at the end, jumped high in joy!

"Whoa! Surya, your jump cracked the floor!" Koma said. He was waiting outside the lab for the whole time. When he heard the news about Surya being the co-ordinator, he too was happy and he came in to offer assistance to him with the ma'am's permission.

"Ohhh, so you boys won't travel alone anywhere huh?" Ms Anne asked.

"Never ever ma'am!" Koma replied to which Surya smiled.

"Okay, So, I think that's good. But, have this principle in your books too. I never even signed the first experiment till now in your book Koma!"

"Ma'am, we never had classes this year! This is the third working day of the school this academic year!"

"I'm saying about the last year Koma... Not this year's. You haven't submitted your observations for your eleventh grade till now and you speak on as the twelfth grader, the senior most student of Krya huh?"

"Past is past ma'am... Let's forget those!" Koma said with an awkward smile.

"Okay, here's the thing Surya! In order to organise the fresher's party first plan the events you wish to do. I'll leave it to your wish, but on one condition. You need to do two programmes that I tell you."

"Okay ma'am."

"Now, I want you to do a speech on the fresher's day. Not as an organiser, but as a student of Krya. You must make the new students *feel good that they're in a great school. You must tell all the achievements our school had made, all the awards we got, all the facilities we have…"*

"I get it ma'am. You want me to tell all lies. That's all right? I get it!"

"Well, I hate to tell this, but yes. You got the point."

"…and the second programme, ma'am?" Surya asked.

"I need you to do a skit."

"What?"

"A skit… A story written, directed, dialogues, acted by you!"

"Ma'am! A full skit?"

"Yes! Only if you do that, I can tell everyone that you did this skit in such a small time and show your talents as an organiser to the other teachers and could show them that you're capable of being SPL."

"Ma'am, I want to ask something ma'am."

"Yes ask."

"Isn't this wrong ma'am? You supporting me to become SPL? What if someone else is really worthy of it? Isn't this like you were only showing me as the one and only person in the class? Isn't it looking like you're favouring for only my good? Isn't this the same way, Mrs Susan favoured Jacob?"

"You don't understand Surya. I'm not supporting only you. I was ready to support the one who's really worthy of it. When you did your march past, I found out that you could become capable of it. During the practise I've seen how well you acted, thinking that I was even more comfortable with the thought of you being the SPL, even more, when you told me how much you'd love to take on the duty of SPL, I really knew that you could become one. So, when we found a performer, we offer him a stage. And all I'm doing now is the same. Favouring someone on considering their talents is not wrong Surya."

"Now I'm clear ma'am. I'm not feeling guilty."

"Dude! Are you this much an honest person?" Koma asked laughing.

"Well, sometimes!" Surya said.

"Okay ma'am, I'll accept for both. May I go ma'am?"

"Yes… you may. All the best Surya!"

Surya walked out of the lab happily and walked through the corridors briskly. He nearly jumped while walking to control his joy. He on thinking about being joyful a lot got remembered on how he ran through the corridors of C.B.W. in the same manner, after seeing Shivani for the first time. Surya's joy increased again on thinking about it. He too then remembered how Shivani looked when they were about to perform the Heal the World performance on stage. She wore a pure milky white dress that even had wings in it, where she held a wand in her hands, wore a crown in her head, and stitched her tight to

Surya's heart, as he watched her open mouthed that day, even during the song performance, where he stopped singing for a moment on her entry. Surya then laughing about it asked Koma.

"Why do all the good things ever happen to me in physics lab Koma?"

"Why're you saying that?"

"That's a long story. I'll tell you later. Now come on! Chop-chop, we need ourselves people to help." Surya said.

The boys reached the classrooms and found it to be empty. They saw only few girls sitting and eating in the back corner of the room. They were laughing so loud on a hilarious topic that all of their laughs echoed and vibrated the whole room. Surya went in fast as if he was sure about what he was doing. Straight away he went and called,

"Maha, I seriously need your help."

Maha was the person we've already seen. Well, she was of course the student of Krya, let's not widen our guesses till 21st of May 1996, yet, Maha was already encountered when Surya sat in the aftermath of the first blow. Remember when Surya sat in the classrooms silently awaiting for the chemistry test to be conducted? That moment he saw Maha. She was the one who laughed hilariously and completely carefree. She was the one whom Surya saw and thought about why his life turned out bad by then. Surya knew that Maha was among the toppers of the class, after Ajay. Somehow Ajay always had hold of the first mark. Well, keeping in mind that Surya's got to speak about Krya, Surya wanted Maha to help him with that and also, he wanted her guidance as an old student of Krya to let him conduct the Fresher's party.

"Oh, yes Surya tell me." Maha replied.

"Maha, I'm now the co-ordinator for the fresher's party that's going to be conducted next week same day. I want you to help me. I need you to compere the party and I need you to act in the play that's going to be there and finally, I need you to tell me what the best things about our school are!"

"Whoa! All this at a time?"

"Yes, I could've given you the speech part. But, ma'am told me to do it myself."

"Okay, no problem Surya. I'll write the speech for you, meanwhile you write the play. Tomorrow we'll exchange the both and we'll select the characters. Give me the events list and I'll prepare for compering."

"Thanks, Thanks a lot Maha! I owe you a big time favour."

"You're welcome Surya!"

"Maha, Let's decide the casts of our play tomorrow itself, alright?"

"Hmm, alright Surya! No problem. First you finish the script."

"Yea, that I'll do it. I'll take care of that! Thanks Maha!"

"Anytime!"

"BOO!" Surya suddenly said while he saw our old friend Vidya, who silently was reading a novel. Surya always did that as she'd jump each and every time Surya scared her. Even now she jumped. Surya laughed on seeing it and said, "Oh, Hey Vidya, you're here too? How come I haven't heard any of your voice till now?"

"That's because I'm reading you MORON! Don't scare me like that again! I might get a heart attack!"

"First it should be there to attack." Surya mumbled.

"What?"

"Nothing, take medicines, you look weak." Surya said and both Surya and Koma laughed and ran.

That day, Surya and Koma planned a lot on the events. They spoke to all and they thought about all. Since the fresher's party were done only by the twelfth graders, they didn't have a lot of work to roam around the school. They just asked their fellow classmates from other sections and planned the events. Surya was also surprised to know that Koma was going to do a dance in the event. Surya laughed about it at first and enlisted Koma's name too. Both the friends then by the evening started to depart from the school. Koma as usual went up to his bus, number 16 and kept his bag and returned. Then they went near Surya's bus, number 20, and stayed there and talked.

"Surya, it's been a while, I wanted to ask you something."

"Yea, ask."

"*Where the hell is Jean?*"

"*She's of course in some bus by now! She came to school didn't you see her?*"

"*No, I'm asking where she is in our gang. You, I and she were close friends remember? Suddenly she's stopped talking with us dude!*"

"*Man, I don't have answers for that. It's from that Chemistry lab exam she's not speaking much. At first I stopped speaking you knew that. But later, she never joined us.*"

"*What is it with these girls dude? How come they be so free to talk with us, then so occupied to not even see us? How in the damn world is this possible bro?*"

"*Everything's possible when you speak about girls, dude. Leave that sick topic!*"

"*Hey, how did you tell me that the girl Priyanka was only friend to you? She seemed really caring. I accept, I told her that even I had doubts. But how do you surely say it's just friendship?*"

"*The thing is, you don't know about Priyanka. She's just the way our class Maha is. They both are like rain. They'll shed water for everyone. Whereas we boys are like ATM. We only give money if they produce the right card.*"

"*Good concept, bad example Surya.*" Koma said.

"*Well, that's the proof that I made up the phrase!*"

"Again a bad counter... Okay, hope God saves you from yourself. Bye! I got to go!" Koma went as he heard the physical master's whistle.

"Bye Buddy!"

"Hey Surya, how was your day?" Priyanka asked. They were walking by the roads of I.E.C. Township, after the bus ride from school.

"You wouldn't believe what had happened Priyanka! I'm the co-ordinator for the fresher's day!" Surya exclaimed.

"Wow! That's great to hear! So, what're your plans?"

"First I must change the damn events in it. It's just our assembly with the seniors' dance. I'm going to include more events and cancel of the assembly events, most of them."

"Okay, do whatever you want. But, do it well Surya! Best of luck!"

"Yeah thanks Priyanka! Ok I really have to go now. Good bye!"

"Bye Surya!"

Surya went on to his home. He then told his mom about what happened in the school that day and straight away went to his room. There he started to think about the programs that can attract each and every audience. He started writing them down when he found promising choices. Later, he remembered the play that he had to direct. So, for the play, Surya didn't think much. He had already done a play for the English class which was titled, 'Affection Kills Addiction'. Surya had a look at it.

It was a story of a village boy, who joins in a prestigious college in merit, where he gets into drugs due the death of his father, and becomes addicted to it due to the increased compulsion from his college friends. One day, the college management finds drugs in the boy's room where at the very instant. The boy gets into trouble in class, where he starts jumping on the benches and insults the professor very much. When the management decides to expel him, seeing his true condition as an innocent intelligent boy, a professor in the college deciphers on whose drugs they were, speaks with the college's disciplinary council and saves the boy from expulsion and cure him from addiction.

"Okay! The casts are..." Surya noted down the casts. These days Surya was selfish. He wanted him to be seen. So, he took the character of the professor who saves the boy. Well, at least he by then recognised that he got to take down the opportunities. Not wait for them. It's necessary in today's world. Nobody ever likes to give. Then what's the need to wait anyway?

"Surya! Come on let's eat!" Surya's mom called.

"Yes, coming!" Surya said and went.

By the time, Surya went out and saw that his father had already come. He said nothing and started to wash his hands and sat down on the floor. He wanted to tell about the day's happening to him and that he has a good chance of becoming the SPL of Krya CBSE. The room seemed so silent and Surya's dad's brows were shrunk to the centre of his fore head.

"What happened dad?" Surya asked.

"What's there to happen? Nothing."

"Something's happened. Say what?"

"I don't know for how many days Surya! For how many days should I find the posts of you and your filthy marks?"

Surya fell silent.

"What's your problem Surya? I thought of not to tell you this, but you're making me speak all about it. Why aren't you getting good marks?"

"Dad, I'm reading dad! I just don't know, I couldn't remember the things at that moment in the exams. I am trying, but it's just..."

"... Not enough." Surya's dad interrupted. "You don't know, your mom may tell you are reading all the time, you may read all the time, but if that is so, where's the result? Maybe I'm wrong, but to me, what you read, your input is not at all enough. You are not giving the necessary works that are required. Always do smart work. Only hard work along the right direction could bring you success. That's all I can say. You are your own judge. If you think you're working hard that's ok." Surya's dad told.

Surya was silent. In this mood of him, SPL news won't be much pleasing him. So, Surya dropped the topic, stopped eating and went to his home. Surya's mom was helpless against the family's condition. Everywhere there seemed no happiness. Most of the food's gone waste all the time. Nobody ate well. The family's peace was lost. Maybe every average student's house becomes like this when he comes to twelfth grade or whether this was the curse to Surya, there lived a fear among the people of the family all the time.

Twelfth grade is always a terror to many living students out here. Every relation remembers a student who's studying in a twelfth grade. Indian schooling and education systems have created hype through these exams. These exams were the life and death battle of the student, though the government doesn't portray so. So, on the grade, that's leading to the life and death battle, on the grade where every relation remembers, is the grade where Surya's standing. This made the whole family, fear about the performance of Surya too.

Well, coming to our story, Surya was exhausted on these topics. He desperately needed success. So, Surya worked hard on selecting the people the next day.

"Maha, I've prepared the skit. Take whatever role you want and let's select the others. This is the script." Surya said.

"Yea okay Surya, now here's the speech." Maha said and gave a paper to Surya.

"What! State level chess championship winner from our school?"

"Yes!" Maha said with a big smile.

"Why should the credit go to the school?"

"Because the champion happens to be our school student."

"Come on Maha, they wouldn't have taught about chess and all."

"Maybe, but he belongs to Krya right? For the record, there is coaching for chess too."

"Alright whatever! I got to tell a lie! I'll say it!" Surya said and went.

"So, dude, what're the events." Koma asked.

"A speech from me, from teachers, from our correspondent, two solo dance performances, one group dance performance, one skit, one vote of thanks." Surya said.

"Alright! Who're the dancers?"

"You in the male solo, and Jean for the female solo." Surya said.

"What! Jean?"

"YES! How did you? When did you speak?"

"Yesterday."

"She speaks?!"

"Yes dude, I was the one who stopped talking right, so, I again started speaking and she gave me ideas too, but as much didn't work out for the time given, I've just selected dances. She said she'll dance so, I've written her name. Siya and some other girls are doing a group dance, and the skit... We all are doing. You, me, Maha, Vidya, and Dwarakesh, Vishnu, Ashwin, Suresh, Mohan and some others too." Surya said.

"*Okay, dude, this is the performance I'm telling about. When are we practicing?*"

"*From today. From the last period.*"

"*Last period is... MATHS!*"

"*WHAT!!!?*" Surya exclaimed. He, being the co-ordinator had to ask permission to the teacher, while taking the students to practices.

"*Not the first day itself!*" Surya cursed.

The time arrived. Surya was waiting for our beloved skinny teacher, Mr Xavier. He was prepared well and ready with the cast members to go on for the practise. To his luck, all the people of the crew belonged to the same class. So, it'd be a mass bunk if Surya took them away from the class. He was nervous to speak about this with Mr Xavier. Then as usual, with just the delay of two minutes, Mr Xavier entered the class.

"*Good evening Sir!*" *Everyone in the class wished in chorus and stood up.*

"*Sit down students.*" *Mr Xavier told in his husky silent voice. Everybody sat, except Surya, for he had to ask the permission. Mr Xavier, on seeing him frowned and asked.*

"*Can't you understand English?*"

Surya's anger rose as a volcano. Mr Xavier's mocking irritated him. Yet, with the need to continue the practise, he asked Mr Xavier.

"Sir, it's not that. Due to the fresher's party, some of our class students are doing performances in that day sir. They've told us to practise in the last hour of the day sir, so, if you kindly give us the permission to leave, we'll practise sir."

"So, all you want is my permission."

"Yes sir."

"What if I don't give it?"

"Sir, we won't have any other time to practise sir."

"How about the games hour?"

"Sir, it was yesterday sir and they gave us permission only today. That's why I'm asking Sir."

"Always having an answer in the pockets eh? But, how should I give the permission? I'm going to teach an important topic in the class."

"Sir, we'll write it down later."

"Oh! Then you're only cared about writing it down. Not learning. Aren't you?"

"Sir, it's not like that sir. It's just that the party is in next Monday and we have only few days to prepare sir."

"So you have to go at any cost?"

"Yes sir."

"Then why did you ask permission? You have to go right? Why should you ask permission of this old teacher? You've already made a decision and why do you still want to ask permission for name's sake?" Mr Xavier scrutinized Surya. He showed no mercy. For each of his words Surya's anger rose. Yet tolerating them, he was standing bearing all the heat.

"Okay, go! Take all your refugees too!" Mr Xavier ordered.

"Thank you sir." Surya said, bearing all the irritations.

"How many are coming with you?"

"13 Sir." Surya said.

"So, with you are without you?"

"Including me Sir!"

"No wonder 13's an unlucky number." Mr Xavier said.

Surya's face changed like a gorilla's as Mr Xavier told the comment. He was referring him as unlucky and was teasing the whole group. Yet, how can a child fight with a teacher? So, Surya silently went, while some if the students in the class laughed.

The insult Mr Xavier gave geared up Surya. Surya was so determined to make the drama a success. So, he was a little hard on his friends. He taught them how he wanted the expressions, he asked them their suggestions to improve the play, and he monitored their performances keenly. On the other hand, he saw both the dance performances on every day's end and even the group dance was checked. On the whole, he was making a drastic progress with the preparations. Later, it was Friday evening. The school was off on Saturdays and this was the last day they could prepare. Surya didn't want to add any more scrutiny to the students. He just did one final rehearsal and left them all free. While only Maha had to tolerate him as she too had the big role in the fresher's day.

"Surya, I told you, let's keep the skit in the very end. Only then they'll wait for it!"

"I don't know, maybe they'll be really tired with the speeches and dances itself. They couldn't wait for the whole play in the end. Nobody would see it Maha!"

"Trust me Surya, dramas are meant to be in the end. It's how they work. Let's keep it in the end itself." Maha said.

"Alright. If you say so."

"Prepared for the speech?"

"Nope."

"What! Surya it's been four days and could you do it in the weekends itself?"

"For your info, I lost that damn paper!"

"WHAT!"

"It's because of the play's scripts Maha! My room is messed up with all those papers that I lost this one in the bundle."

"Can I write it now for you?"

"Oh! Don't, I'll take care of it. Now, we've discussed everything right? Let's go home. I've already asked you so much!"

"Oh, it's alright Surya!"

"How come you're so nice to everyone Maha? Seriously teach that to me! I need it, especially with a teacher with a vengeance."

"This is nothing Surya! I have to learn more too."

"You're such a rare person. Anyways, the speech is my duty; I'll take care of that Maha thank you, bye!" Surya said.

"So, Surya, shall we go?" Koma said, while he came, picking up Surya's bag.

"Yes bro. We can. Thanks." Surya and Koma walked slowly to their buses.

"Can't believe I'm doing all these. School to me was a paradise Koma. I loved my school back then. Those days were the happiest day in my life! But now, all are just happening on some logic and I'm just seeing them without any reaction."

"I don't know what to say. Don't hit me with serious dialogues dude; I don't know how to react."

"Ha-ha" Later both the friends reached their buses and eventually reached to their homes. Surya then spent the weekend preparing for the fresher's day.

Chapter 29: The Fresher's day!

"*G*ood Morning to my dear fresher's, my dearest classmates and the most lovable and precious teachers and staffs of the greatest school ever known!" Maha said in the Krya's auditorium echoing, clear and loud.

The auditorium was filled with the new students of Krya. The school had a lot of new admissions this year that nearly all the seats looked filled. With new heads that Krya has not seen before. They all looked excited and anxious on their first day in Krya, just how Surya's batch looked in their fresher's day. There were a lot of sounds generated during the ceremony's start, which came to an end when Maha started to speak.

"This day last year, we sat in your seats, while the seniors we looked upon were standing here. It's been a beautiful year in Krya for us and we all wish that you people enjoy it too. Without wasting any of your time, let's start the ceremony! I humbly ask our Correspondent Mr Chandrasekhar to welcome the students."

Saying that, Maha went down to the back of the stage and saw Surya and the whole performance crew. Everyone was in their costumes and was looking nervous. Surya was with Koma and Jean. The trio were finally back how they used to be and were having fun.

"Of all the people, the co-ordinator is laughing down here." Maha said.

"Come on Maha! With you here, why should I worry?"

"Oh, Surya. Come on let's start the shows. Please come and see."

"Alright."

While the correspondent finished the speech, the crowd gave a good ovation. Surya and Maha looked over it and Maha then took over the mike. Later after every people spoke, it was Surya's turn.

"Now that you've all heard about our faculties and with our honourable correspondent Sir, let's hear it from the guy one among us, Surya!" Maha said. And while she was coming off the mike, Surya thanked her for the intro and went up to the mike.

He thought in his mind, "It's now or never, Surya!"

"Hello everybody!" Surya said it firm and loud. "I'm Surya, from the twelfth grade. This is a very special day among us twelfth graders. Because, this would be the last celebration we would conduct in Krya CBSE. Though it may look heart-breaking, it is like a big conclusion for a tremendous tale. Good tales have good ending, some may not, and I accept that too. Well, In the case of Krya, we had a pretty good roller coaster ride. As a roller coaster gets exciting during their ups and extremely thrilling on the downs, our life at Krya, though it is just of one year, was really pleasing. When we look into the pages of our

Diary, if we had one, each and every day would have been something different from the other one.

Enjoyments extend exponentially while we were at Krya. Just the walk from the bus, to our classes, takes us into heaven and would lure all our concentration at one place. That concentration, when we decide to use it, would gift us with the sweetest fruit on earth. I'm not a rank holder, I'm certainly not among the toppers but a place like Krya had given me a physical and as well as a mental power to lead a successful career. You're about to see the most different teachers of all time. You would be redefining the phrase of school while you are at Krya.

As seniors, the story we all would tell about Krya, is this. There was this boy, who went lost in the Jungle. He was scared for he heard loud noises of elephants trumpeting, lion roaring, snakes sizzling and birds chirping. He was scared and he started running, running wildly in the direction that he saw. Suddenly, a phoenix bird stood before him. It was so beautiful that the moment the boy saw the bird; he forgot that he was lost and he calmed his mind. Something told him that it was this place, which he was destined to. It was here he had to come. It was this place that was his destination from day one. The phoenix came near him. It spread its wings in the beaming sunlight, the boy saw himself lift from the ground and float. Then with one swing with the wing, the boy and the bird both shot up at the sky and from up there the boy saw his home and was happier to see his mom waiting for him. Then the phoenix bird flew with him to his house, and dropped him near the meadow that reached his house. The boy, after seeing his mom, ran to her and hugged her. When he turned, he saw the bird missing. He just wished thanks to the bird in his heart and went on to his mom.

We twelfth graders are just like the boy. We were lost before. We never knew where to go and we were running without any aim. Then we reached Krya. Well no, Krya reached out to help us. Krya became our destination. It enlightened us and showed our home, showed our success. While we pursue, it stays with us and when we achieve this success, we'd have it gone, to help the others who ran through the forest. Well, you guys have just seen Krya, you too like us, have seen the phoenix only now. You people have a great distance to fly with Krya. Let's fly together and let's all fly high!

WELCOME TO KRYA FOLKS! And this is Surya, signing off!" Surya said out loud in the end. He then heard the whole audience's ovation. The speech that was just made up on stage was really outstanding to the people at Krya. Everyone was laughing backstage. Some were really proud. Especially Koma.

"Dude! WOW!! This speech was so awesome!" Koma shouted.

"You really can speak my friend." Jean said.

"Thank you!"

"Surya, what did you just do now?" Maha asked smiling.

"What? Come on guys this is just a simple thing." Surya said shyly.

"You know what? Our correspondent asked me whether you were the SPL. He also said that he liked your speech and that he himself thought that you were the SPL of the school. Congrats Surya."

"Hey come on. Only half the plan is over. Still the skit and other performances are there. Now come on. Let's go."

Later, Surya watched over the performances happily. The group dance was enlightening the fresher's and the seniors in the audience and Jean's dance bought a real big beat to the show. Later, it was Koma's performance. Nearly each and every person of the twelfth grade looked up in awe for Koma never even landed a foot in the stage, while he walked, jumped, rolled, moonwalked through the whole stage with his super freestyle moves. Surya and Jean and nearly the whole students were shocked to see the energy Koma had.

"Wow, what a great speech!" Ms Anne said.

"Ma'am, you told me to tell a lie, and I did with a story that's it!"

"Hmm… you're a pretty good liar. The surprise here is that our Koma too has talents!" Ms Anne said.

"Yes Ma'am! So, how's the show?" Surya asked in surprise.

"Really, really good Surya! I'm really proud of your work. Guess what, from the speech you gave, nearly the whole lot of teachers were amused and they have been speaking about you being worthy to become the SPL."

"Wow!!!!!!!! Ma'am, are you serious! Wow! I can't believe this! Tell me I'm not dreaming!" Surya shouted.

"Okay, I know you're excited. But, still you got to finish the job you've started. So, come on now focus and Koma's getting to the finish. Start the skit. Now, this is really important. This skit will identify you. This is the final blow you got to give to the teachers. Make my works count." Ms Anne said and left to the seats.

"Wow, What a fabulous performance Koma! Everybody give some cheers to our Koma!" Maha said. The crowd too gave a big ovation. Not only his central incisors, but all the teeth of Koma were pointing out now. He just loved the way he was cheered. He bowed down and went backstage, while Maha continued.

"Now, we've seen some good performances today. We did hope to have rocked you my dear fresher's. There had been enjoyment. Now, let's hold on to our seats, for the final performance of the day, for the one drama we had set up, to help you choose between the good and bad in this life. Let's hear it from the crew of "Affection kills addiction", directed by Surya.

The play went on as planned to Surya. The crew acted so very well, that it was astonishing Ms Anne and she was praising it to the other teachers about Surya's work in it, which went gossiping throughout the teachers present, watching over the really good play. Well, the disadvantage of gossiping is that the news goes to everyone.

The play was concluded and got a great response from the audience. Surya was praised by every teacher and even the principal of Krya CBSE told him that this was a great play that it deserved to be on the cultural fest that year. Surya was so very happy and enjoyed the success with Koma, Jean and Maha and everyone in the crew and in the performance that day. The people had Ms Anne praising them and she told how Surya was now deserved to be in the minds of the teachers and it's a 99.99% sure that Surya would become the SPL. Well, hands of God did have the 0.01% chance.

"Yay!! Surya, this is a victory to all of us dude! Everybody won, and no losers! Finally did a BIG performance in this school! YAY!!" Koma was shouting in enjoyment. Both the friends were in the Van stand and were literally jumping on to the success that they both had. Surya and Koma had their lips stretch limitless. After a while, Jean came to them smiling.

"Surya, Koma I want to tell something to you."

"What's that Jean?" Koma asked.

"I'm sorry."

"What? Why?" Surya asked puzzled.

"It's something that I should've told you. I was really just moving on with the other girls of the class while you were upset Surya. You see, from the time I was from the Emirates, I was so worried about my parents. I missed them so hard, that I can't stop worrying every

now and then. When I was with you both, all the crazy things you both did, lifted me up, I felt free of the homesickness whenever I was there with you both. But, after the lab exams, when you became sad and when you stopped speaking, I was reminded of the same sorrow. I didn't want that to be repeated. That's when I went to the girls, they could never be you two, but they at least made me forget for a little time. But last week when you called and told me that you want some ideas and participants for the performance, that's when I realized that I too was a dancer. From then, when I was practising, I never felt much happy. I really was back to form and just when I came back to you all during the rehearsals, I only then found out what I was really missing. I just missed all the fun while I was with you too. I shouldn't have gone. I'm sorry for that, alright?" Jean said.

Both Surya and Koma were smiling at Jean while she said this. When she finished saying these, she looked at the two smiling. Both the boys by the time she looked started laughing their lungs out. Jean looked confused at why they were laughing. She at first was confused and later the boys' laugh caught hold of Jean too, for she too started laughing.

"Okay, why are you laughing?" Koma asked Jean.

"Both of your laughter were hilarious that's why. Why were you two laughing?"

"Because of you and what you just said now!" Surya said.

"Why?"

"Come on J… are we this formal for asking sorry?"

"Will you ask sorry in family? Come on! We are three souls in one body." Koma said.

"Thanks guys. But, why didn't both of you come and ask me before? Why didn't you ask even when we were speaking during the rehearsals?"

"Oh, we thought you had amnesia and we would never again take a risk to speak with you!" Koma said and started to run. Well Jean just smiled and said,

"Anyways, bye guys, thank you for coming into my life." Jean said and started leaving to her bus. While she went, Priyanka came by.

"Well Well Well! Look who's here! The star of Krya CBSE." She said with a smile.

"Oh come on! Who told you now itself?" Surya asked.

"Just that I'm in the next building it doesn't mean I'm alienated from you."

"Well, I did do well today!" Surya said.

"Hmm, I sure would love to hear it Surya!"

"Wait!" Koma suddenly came in between them.

"I must ask something to you Ms Priyanka." He asked. Priyanka though surprised asked him what that was.

"I'm having a really big confusion. I'm sorry, but please do answer."

"Okay tell!"

"Are you having any feelings for Surya?" Koma asked bluntly which made Surya and Priyanka shocked.

"Dude! What the hell?! I told you, she never had any feelings for me! Why are you asking it again now?" Surya shouted at Koma.

"Surya! Wait! That question was for me right? I must answer it!" Priyanka replied.

"Now that's the spirit! Tell me please?" Koma asked.

"That depends on how you define the word 'feeling'"

"Well, you know the 'L' word?"

"Well, no."

"That's it?"

"I think that is enough for the answer for your question?"

"Well, it answers, but it's not satisfactory."

"Why?"

"Because, I still feel strange about you being extremely cared about him."

"Oh, so caring is loving?"

"Well, yeah?"

"So, I guess you and Surya are lovers?"

"EWW! That's bad for nearly three fourth of the people in the world!"

"See, when you could care for him and can call it friendship, why shouldn't I call it so?" Priyanka said. Surya was smiling at Koma to which he smiled wanly.

"Alright. Then you win." Koma said and went to his bus. "Thank you for clearing my doubts Ms Priyanka!" He said.

"Thanks for clearing. I nearly spent a whole year making them believe that we're just friends." Surya said.

"Anytime buddy!" Priyanka said as they boarded the bus and sat in their places.

"What's up dude?" Surya said to Nandhu who was already seated in the bus.

"Hey man! What a good day! You really changed the course of the fresher's party!" Nandhu said.

"Thanks bro!"

"So, all well and good, did you read for the tests tomorrow?"

"What tests?"

"Test in Physics, chemistry and maths?"

"WHAT!!!!! ALL OF THEM?"

"YEP!" Nandhu said laughing.

From then, Surya had to go for the race. This is a hurdles race. For each and every step forward, there's a barrier that's got to be jumped on and these barriers comes as fast as we go forward. In order to jump these barriers, the mind must be at peace and it had to be free to concentrate. So, maybe all of the confusions that went up in Surya's head were now cleared just for him to be at peace in his mind to perform well in the race. Yet, there is one question, will Surya be the SPL?

Chapter 30: All that looks bad isn't evil.

*L*ife went so swift and fast from the fresher's day. Each and every day went as fast as sticks stuck in river. They passed away so fast in just a blink of second. Maybe times waits for no one, but it sure does fly when we're always busy. Each and every day twelfth grade students of Krya were constantly attacked with lessons and tests every day. Everyone had to climb a mountain full of stumbling rocks. Where not only climbing is important, but who climbs fast are very much important. These days, nobody can rest, nobody can stop, and nobody can even blink for the time that's travelling in a super highway. Everybody was engaged busily. These days the clear mind-set led Surya perform efficiently. Surya stopped failing in the subjects, he spent more time in learning the salt analysis, he spent more time asking doubts in mathematics though he didn't like Mr Xavier, he spent more time studying in the library, at home, while travelling in the bus to school, while every games and free hour he got, he studied.

All went well and it was the month of august, the time for the announcement of SPL. It was nearly clear to everyone that Surya would become the SPL. Everybody already called him so. Surya though loved hearing that, asked his friends to stop calling him like that. He had planned several good ways to have good functions organised in the school. He prepared on walking styles, speaking styles etc. he nearly started living the life of an SPL. It's now ten a.m. on the nose. The attendant would be there any minute, to call the boy who's going to be the SPL. It was told by Ms Anne that the announcements would be made by the correspondent himself coming to the class.

Surya and Koma were nail-biting for nearly an hour to meet the correspondent and to react on hearing the news from his own voice, to clearly titling Surya as the SPL of Krya CBSE! Then as the time went near, Surya and Koma even had their adrenalines pumped in excitement. Then, they both saw the correspondent of Krya come as Ms Anne said. They both were jumping on seeing him.

"Wow, the proudest moment in my LIFE!" Surya thought.

"Excuse me sir!" The correspondent said. As the correspondent came in, everybody in the class rose. He ordered them to be seated and continued, "My dear students! As you all know, the SPL should have been selected by this time of the year, with the observations of teachers amongst the students around you. So, without wasting any more time, let me tell you something about the boy who's selected as the SPL. I saw him twice. What I remember about this boy was that I saw him in an English play, where he did an extremely well job. Also I was seeing him marching during our sports day months back. I believe he did march well! He might surely be the good SPL this school would ever see. Anyway, our teachers' decision won't be wrong. OF course many had given their opinion in a written letter, that too so unanimously! This was the first ever time all of them accepted for one boy. Think *he must really deserve the post. So, I hereby declare, Jacob as the new School Pupil Leader of Krya CBSE!"*

The whole class clapped. Everyone was shouting 'Yay' for the new SPL, the new leader for the people of Krya, their new official SPL of the school. Jacob went up and looked at the correspondent, shook his hands. Later, the correspondent called out for someone. Then that person entered. She came with a mouth full of smile and with a badge in her hand. The correspondent went and took it in his hands and placed it on the boy's chest. He proudly went up and held it in his chest, the greatest honour for the boy. He, after speaking with the correspondent got the congratulations from the teacher who had brought the badge. Later, Mr Correspondent said,

"Students, though there is an investiture ceremony that's going to be held soon, now I would like you to show our SPL, Mr Jacob! He is the gem amongst you, to whose leadership qualities, the post is delivered. Thank you, have your enjoyments in your free times guys! Good bye!"

Krya now had their SPL. They had chosen him. He's the most notable boy in school! He's the guy who's worthy enough to take on the responsibilities; he is the guy who's going to change the course of all the programs of Krya. He's going to lift up the whole fate of Krya! Well, we did see what had happened. The new SPL is selected and that's final. But, what happened to our boy? Where's the 99.99% surety? Where's the prize for all the hard work? Well, to know that, let's see what had happened. We do know that Surya, being the worthy one for the SPL went gossiping through the whole teachers' circle. Well, the news went on eventually to the one that needed to be told now. It went to Mrs Susan. She was extremely uncomfortable for Surya to be nominated as SPL. She became so angry when Surya left the drama crew. Well actually she was happy for him to leave the crew without fighting for the role, but the real thing was what Surya had told while leaving. What he said was, "I'm way beyond these people ma'am. So, no thank you."

Mrs Susan heard this and thereafter she was angry on Surya. Well, we know what would result in the anger. Mrs Susan went on planning to get Jacob the SPL post. She couldn't think of anybody. Surya went on the hype with all the teachers and he really was selected as the SPL. But, what fate made possible was that, the letter, containing Surya as the SPL was flipped by Mrs Susan. She rubbed off Surya's name and had put Jacob's name in it. Till then, nobody knew this had happened, only after the announcement in the class, when the correspondent had sent out the circular to the teachers in congratulating in selecting the SPL, everybody knew that it was now Jacob, who's the SPL.

When the news arrived at the teachers' stations, Ms Anne went furious. She was angry that the teachers had made a decision beyond her proofs of Surya being worthy. She went directly and spoke with the teachers.

"Ma'am what happened ma'am?" She asked to a teacher.

"Why Anne?"

"I did tell you all to elect Surya as the SPL. Didn't I? I did prove him that he could be worthy. I gave him the big task of fresher's day and it went successfully as never before. This guy Jacob had never even attended any of the rehearsals we did in his play. When a guy doesn't even come to a pre-informed program how worthy is he to conduct new things? Why ma'am? Am I that much inferior in your minds that what I tell doesn't even go through your ears? Who am I? I'm also a faculty in this school! And I too have the equal status of you all. Just because I'm the youngest, don't underestimate me ma'am" She roared to all the teachers present there.

"Anne calm down!" a teacher from the crew said.

"How am I supposed to be calm ma'am? I promised that boy that for his talent he will be the SPL. His interests were high on achieving it and he did a pretty good job in a very less time that even we teachers would stumble upon! How will I ever see his face again? Won't I be a betrayer in his eyes? Won't I be a filthy animal who could break a promise? Let him be a twelfth grader ma'am, but he still is a child. It's not so soon that he could face big failures. He also has his Goddamn exams coming. Won't this affect him? If you hadn't promised me I too wouldn't have promised him!" Ms Anne said. She was very emotional.

"Look, Anne. We ourselves were thinking about telling you. We by the morning knew that instead of Surya, Jacob was selected. We too were as shocked as you when we heard it. Later, when we thought about how this could've happened, only then it stroke to my mind that it was Mrs Susan who was to sign the letter last and she volunteered to submit it to the correspondent. Also, we did know that Jacob and Susan were family friends and that led up to the conclusion that she did change the name finally in the official letter."

"Even after finding that it was her, were you sitting quiet?"

"We're not cruel people Anne. We went to her and asked about it. But what happened was she started shouting at us for accusing her and she created a big scene in the corridors that ruined all of our names. She acted as if we were accusing her of murder and that she was born innocent."

"Why didn't you complain this to the correspondent ma'am?"

"We did go. He said all official records were already printed with Jacob as the SPL and that it can't be changed now. He was not at all serious with the topic. He was telling that it was just a formality to have an SPL and he said us not to come fighting for anybody. We were just helpless. I'm sorry Anne." Ms Anne after hearing this calmed down. She then apologized to the madam.

"Oh… I'm so sorry ma'am. The circular raised my temper ma'am. Sorry if what I did hurt you!"

"Oh don't worry Anne. Even I would've been as angry as you if my works went unappreciated. By the way, where is Surya? Did you meet him after the announcement?"

"Not yet ma'am. I'm really, really afraid actually. I can't face him ma'am." Ms Anne said.

We did leave Surya jumping didn't we? Well, let's go back to the class after the announcement was made. Though every student had called Surya as the SPL first, on hearing the official announcement went up to Jacob, calling him an SPL and cheering him. Three people in the class only knew what Surya went through and how he'd be feeling now. It was Koma, Maha and Jean. The trio looked at Surya just when Jacob's name was told. They all saw what Surya's reactions were, and for the first time, they saw Surya very much in trouble.

They saw his eyes trembling. It rushed left and right. His look went down. He always drummed his table when he was angry. He did them now too. He breathed heavily, as this was the failure that he had got on so much hardships he had faced. Surya went on with his brows shrunk. He rested his head on keeping his hands in the table and looked on to the floor. But whatever he did, fold his hands, look left, look right, see down, rest his heads in his arms, even on just shaking his legs, his inner pain was reflected through his eyes. Surya couldn't tolerate the blow. He had been struck for the third and final time. Koma tried to hold Surya's shoulders, to which he shook himself to remove it. He cracked his teeth in anger. He once looked at Maha, Koma and Jean. They too worked hard with him. "Koma and Jean were doing their performances, helped me in mine. But what Maha did was extra-ordinary. Actually, even she would've deserved the SPL title. But, just because I had brought her with me, they too now got my curse. A curse that's supposed to be there for sinners of the seven lives, a curse that had to be given for a man who betrayed his own country, a curse that had to be given for a criminal, who would even dare to kill his own mother. That was the curse given to me, to face failures in every part of life. Maybe I was a sinner in my previous birth, to whose sins I'm suffering. What a sick life!" Surya thought all these while he heard nothing that anybody said. He just went out of the class suddenly and went to the restroom.

There was a mirror in the rest room. Surya was constantly watching it. His emotions were wavering from anger, to sadness, to hatred. He seriously hated even the image of him in the mirror. He just turned away. Later, he saw again. This time, his real senses came in flowing past the anger. His heart broke and Surya mourned deeply. This was probably the worst failure he would have ever faced. This really broke his heart even more. He went on and on thinking about the failure and cried and cried and cried. When just a job gets neglected we'd feel terrible. When we pursued hard for a job, executed all the plans, got a promising tone of success, and when we suddenly face failure in it, how would we describe our sadness? Well words are so inferior to the level of Sadness Surya faced. What is the point of life when what we always see is sorrow and what that becomes too is out of our hands? Well, those questions would be good if they were left unanswered. Surya wasn't punished. He was being taught. He had to be known about the fact. It'd take a miracle for Surya to realise that. So, there the miracle happened.

"Surya?" A voice came in echoing through the restroom doors that made Surya get into his senses. Though he managed to wipe off the tears, it did come out without his control. His visions went blurred with the *tears that went rolling down in his chin. He couldn't recognise who that was. He again wiped it hard and was shocked to see the person who was calling him.*

"Mr Xavier? Sir... I'm... sorry... I... I..." Surya's voice trembled for he was in utter shock and disappointment.

"Come Surya, let's take a walk." Mr Xavier called Surya.

"Ye... Yes Sir..."

"Now do wipe off your face. I can't see your eyes properly and I'm sure as hell that you too can't see."

"Yes sir." Surya went and washed his face and came back to Mr Xavier when they both started for a walk.

"What is your favourite place in the school Surya?"

"Sir, but..."

"Don't think for few minutes. Just answer my questions and hear me out will you?"

"Yes sir."

"So, now what's your favourite place?"

"The canteen Sir! Obviously."

"Ha-ha... Come Surya. Let's go there."

"Sir, but the class..."

"It is my class Surya, I'm sure they're having a good time. Don't worry. Let's go if you don't mind!"

"No sir, not at all!"

"Okay, So... I guess what happened today was the most sad thing you've ever faced huh?"

"Maybe... There's been a lot of Fails in my life that I lost count sir!"

"Why do you think you're failing Surya?"

"...because I'm born to fail, so that others can achieve Sir."

"Look Surya, let me tell you one thing. Life was never destined to anybody Surya. Everybody's life is stitched into grids as in a bandage cloth. It's our choices and actions, that makes us travel through these grids and create the path of our life. Our life, being just the one strand in the cloth, is intersected by many of other strands that comes in and goes out. The way that strand and our strand travel, is the experience of our life with that person. It may be good it may be bad, depending on the both of you. When you keep on think that you're a bad strand, you'd never end up having a good experience with everyone."

"Sir, you are telling me that..."

"Remember the things that I'm going to tell now Surya. There are three things as an adult you must know. First, know who you are and what you want. Because, when we don't even know what we want how

are we supposed to do what's right? Second, know your surroundings and know how the people are behaving around you. See what favours them, what irritates them, what they're actions are and how they behave. Thirdly, do whatever's necessary to stay out of trouble or get the most good out of your observations. All right? Things which are right or wrong, changes over time Surya. Didn't we live in an era where small children were married before? Now aren't we living in the time where those were abolished? Man is the worst animal on the surface of the earth Surya. He changes himself and the whole society time to time. Never look at others Surya, It'd send you to the land of the lost. Always look at the one who's inside you. Follow him, for you'd finally be happier. Now, as we've reached the canteen, what would you like to eat?" Mr Xavier said and went on to buy the samosas for him and Surya.

Surya thought to himself. All he said had more meaning from it. Than the meaning, he did realize every point Mr Xavier had told. Xavier himself was Surya's enemy before. Though he never said anything about it, Surya himself thought to be so. He is a stern person, but in no way he did bad things. He looked bad to Surya's opinion. He judged him by his looks, just like how Dhanvita judged Surya. Both of them never observed. Perhaps observation is really necessary before actions. Surya thought of understanding whatever Mr Xavier told. He thought about the failures that he faced. "He said me know what I want. What I wanted was not to learn chemistry before. I hated it from within that what I planned was just to get it in my mind than learning it, resulting me failing that subject. Later, unnecessarily I fought with Mrs Susan. She not only favoured Jacob, but my actions, made her deny me my success. I should've been more polite when I knew how she and Jacob were close. I shouldn't have made the comment when I left. Maybe that's the thing that triggered her. I should've observed more. I should've acted according to the situation. Mr Xavier's right!" Mr Xavier, while Surya was thinking all these, came by the table with the samosas.

"Also Surya, when you encounter failure, don't look at them alone. It's just a result of unlucky outcomes. Look at what you can do to rectify it. If it fails again, Look again and give another try. If that too fails, look at the outcome and rectify it again and again! You must learn from your failures not worry for them! If something doesn't work out for you, forget it and try on something new! Sure there's room for everybody in this world, we just have to find it that's all! Life is only to learn and enjoy my friend!" Mr Xavier said.

"Sir, I was first prepared to do all of these. But, I never got an opportunity. All I faced was failure so suddenly that I couldn't rectify from it. I never got time to find the opportunity to regain my senses Sir."

"Surya, this world is not as beautiful as it looks. There're a lot of mystic invisible forces that surrounds us. They are so naughty that they'd always leave you waiting, if you wait for the opportunity. If you need an opportunity, don't wait. You won't get any. Hunt for your opportunity, find it, kill it, sit above it and taste success with your work. Now eat the samosas and come, I'm going to start the class, let's go!"

Though he spoke little, this was enough for the bump that Surya needed. He thought about everything that Mr Xavier said. He really felt happier in accepting the failures and learn from them. Just a simple key to overcome nearly as many problems we face in life. Just accept and learn. There won't be worries or sorrows or grievances. Than understand this, it is the human's mind to run in search for a paradise, something that exists in only imagination, something that's only a figment somewhere in the corner of our mind, something we could easily call, Fool's Paradise.

Farewell…

*W*e've travelled a lot with Surya. We've seen his life and his friends and his love. But we didn't see what had happened after Mr Xavier's talk with Surya. We don't have to know. That's Surya who's got to decide what should happen in his life from now. Surya had been shown what real life outside a school campus is and he had been given the bump to tackle it. Let Surya find out what life would become thereafter…

Every person needs a bump as Surya had got. Only then everyone would dawn upon in a new sunrise. Everyone would know their own strength to fight upon the biggest and toughest problems in life. Every day as an adult leaves his home he's constantly hit with so many problems. But the teenage problems would be a pleasant story for every individual which is of course now our boy's story. It's when we ourselves adore our own stupidity. Our own mistakes would make us laugh. Our own craziness would make us think, our own decisions would make us admire ourselves. The adolescent age, half an adult, half a child is something everyone had loved. These times, one can never earn back. One can never forget too. It's when your matured mind and childhood mind meet each other. It's the first time you'd want the whole world to look at you. It's when you would find yourself ending up in new messes each and every day. It's when you have the whole universe's energy in your body; mind and soul that could make you do anything that you want! It's the first step to adulthood. Well, what's it?

It's teenage!